"This is a compelling story c rejection and loss to forgivenes Nicola's bravery will undoubtec journeys to fre ....

Ian and Judith Green, Leaders in Community Transformation, Europe

"In this expose, Nicola shames the darkness that tried to destroy her, effectively gifting readers with their own keys of release to freedom and victory." - **Fay Recca, Co-Pastor, Chiesa Emmanuel, Ragusa, Italy**

"Nicola courageously shares her life story with profound grace and kindness; a story of abuse and neglect that could have left her bitter with very visible scars, rather than invisible ones."
Annabel Bateman, Author and Coach, Brisbane, Australia

"Nicola's story will encourage those who have experienced trauma and been broken by life's events and show them that healing and wholeness is possible. Her immense courage resonates throughout; never minimising the challenges or the pain experienced but indicating that there's hope." -**Colleen Walter, Director of Safe and Sound Learning Association, a Training Provider in the ECD (Early Learning Development Sector) South Africa**

"This compelling story tells of Nicola's journey through brokenness and pain to reach the loving arms of God's grace. This is a story that will encourage your faith as you understand how much God loves those who are rejected by this world and how far He'll go to bring them to Himself."
Meredith Resce, Australian Author

"Nicola has shared the depths of her vulnerable childhood; has given access to you, the reader, to know that God loves, heals and restores those who have been broken in life."
Nick Resce, NLT, Acts Global Churches, Australia

To Jemike,
With lots of Love
Nikki ♡

Phil 1:6

INVISIBLE SCARS

My story of restoration from childhood sexual abuse and trauma

Copyright © 2023 Nicola Rucci

The moral right of the author has been asserted.

Apart from any fair dealing for the purposes of research or private study, or criticism or review, as permitted under Copyright, Design and Patents Act 1998, this publication may only be reproduced, stored or transmitted, in any form or by any means, with prior permission in writing of the publishers, or in any case of the reprographic reproduction in accordance with the terms of licences issued by the Copyright Licensing Agency. Enquiries concerning reproduction outside these terms should be sent to the publishers.

PublishU Ltd

www.PublishU.com

Unless otherwise noted, Scripture quotations are from the New King James Version (NKJV), copyright © 1979, 1980, 1982, Thomas Nelson, Inc., Publishers.

All rights of this publication are reserved.

THANK YOU

To my mum: Thank you for being the champion you are and for being willing to share with me your own healing journey. You are very much loved.

To my husband Gary: Thank you for being my rock and the utmost loyal friend in my life. I thank God every day for you and your unconditional love towards me and our children.

To Nick and Meredith Resce: Thank you for encouraging me to write my story, thank you for always being there, challenging me to become a better version of myself; thank you for being trusted long term friends and for loving me unconditionally.

I'd like to thank Matt Bird and the PublishU team – thank you for giving us all the courage to write our first book. WE DID IT! Now, onto the next one.

I acknowledge all survivors of childhood sexual abuse and trauma. To those of you who haven't yet spoken out and to those who have, yet whose words weren't received well – you are all VICTORIOUS! Be the courageous people you were created to be; rewrite the pages of your future self. Be patient with yourself, go slow in your healing journey and remember that your heart belongs in an intimate space with a trusted few. You are highly valued and very, very loved. God bless you.

CONTENTS

Foreword

Introduction

PART ONE

Chapter 1	Dysfunction Breeds Dysfunction
Chapter 2	The Tapestry of Trauma
Chapter 3	Gary
Chapter 4	Hope in Grief: One day at a Time
Chapter 5	What Research Says

PART TWO

Chapter 6	Our Vulnerability Opens the Doorway to our Healing
Chapter 7	There's a Time for Forgiveness
Chapter 8	Rejection is a Thief: It takes More Than it Gives
Chapter 9	Shame Carries Secrets
Chapter 10	Our Healing Journey isn't a Race to the Finish Line
Chapter 11	What Helped Me, May Help You
Chapter 12	My Faith

About the Author

NICOLA RUCCI

FOREWARD

For over 20 years I ran camps in Toowoomba, Queensland, Australia for teen girls. These camps were for girls in our community, the majority of whom didn't attend church, who were from broken homes and had experienced some form of abuse in their short lifetime. Our team worked hard to provide an environment where the girls could open up, share their pain and heal. On the Saturday night of the camp, we'd have a leader share her story of pain around abuse, rejection or fatherlessness. This was then followed by an apology from my dad or another trusted male adult. He would stand in the gap on behalf of men and apologise to the girls for abusing, rejecting or hurting them in any way at all. It was a powerful three minutes. He would leave the room and we were left with a room of fifty teen girls who were weeping; many would start crying even before the apology was over. Our leaders would then spend the next hour or so just moving among the girls, sitting and listening as they poured out their pain, quite often this was the beginning of a healing journey for them.

I can't help but think that if Nicola had ever attended one of these camps, she too would've been weeping. Her story is one that calls for us to weep, to release the tears of God on earth for the injustices and abuse that she faced; that no little girl should ever have to go through. The sad reality is that her story is the story of thousands of girls in our nation. Many never find healing and limp through life perpetuating the cycle of abuse from one generation to the next.

I first met Nicola in 2020. She invited me to speak at a women's event she was running in her church. She's a respected leader, not only in her church but also in her community. I'm thankful for her courage in sharing her story and the healing journey she's been on. Reading her story has impacted me. She's presented the struggles of her past in such a clear, but practical way; helping the reader to understand what she and so many have gone through with a clear way forward.

Abuse is rampant in our nation. However, many women stay silent due to shame, family pressures and just the lack of awareness (especially in the church) to know how to help and deal with such issues. May this book bring healing to not just women, but men. May it give them courage to speak up and share their story too. May it give readers a deeper understanding of this scourge on our society and what is going on in many homes across our nation. Lastly, may the church find ways to be better equipped so we can be agents of healing in our communities.

Letitia Shelton,

Director of City Women Toowoomba, Author of 'Fighting for our Daughters, The Little Handbook of Disruptive Women Series, The Disruptive Voices of Fijian Women'

INVISIBLE SCARS

NICOLA RUCCI

INTRODUCTION

"Courage doesn't always roar. Sometimes courage is the quiet voice at the end of the day saying, 'I will try again tomorrow.'"

Mary Anne Radmacher

My healing journey wasn't a nice stroll through a beautiful lush green park. It was often messy, confusing and painful. It definitely wasn't a quick healing process, it took time to walk through the traumas of my childhood, unpacking my heart step by step. But I chose to take a risk, being courageous to step into my pain to become a better version of myself, not repeating the same devastating cycle that I grew up in. Even though I still have weaknesses and flaws to walk through today and for the rest of my life, I can smile and laugh with great joy that I'm not that fearful young girl anymore: I'm a grown woman with a loving husband, three adult children, two daughters-in-law (to be) and a grand baby on the way (not to mention an adorable Maltese terrier); all who love me and I them, unconditionally. I can honestly say it was well worth it.

I want to say from the very start that I'm not a professional Psychologist or a qualified counsellor. I am an ordained church minister, wife and mother who feels compelled to tell my story of childhood sexual abuse and trauma.

My story is unique to me and I realise there are thousands of stories like mine. Sadly, I know there are a lot of people who suffer in silence. Perhaps my journey of healing and restoration will offer comfort, hope and wisdom to such people.

We all have a life story. Some of us are at the beginning of our life's story, some of us are somewhere in between and others are coming to the end of their life's story. No matter where we are in our journey, walking it out day-by-day – we hope we'll finish our life far greater and more successful than how we started out. We want the ability to look back with satisfaction; having lived life fully. Sadly, that doesn't happen for everybody. Many people carry the pain, the heartache and the devastation of trauma with them forever; never fully understanding that they can experience breakthroughs and be restored to live abundantly with beautiful memories.

Someone said to me recently that my transparency and bravery in sharing my story helped her to open up about her childhood trauma. She said that for the very first time in her life, she felt the courage to begin sharing her story with a counsellor. This incredible lady is seventy years old and she felt the courage to tell her story for the very first time because I was courageous enough to tell mine. She was courageous enough to listen. She went on her journey of healing at the age of seventy. Wow!

When we're open and transparent, our vulnerability has the power to release others to open up also about their pain. However, it isn't without risks. Some people will view our genuine bravery in being open and speaking out, as a weakness. Others will embrace our story. Some people will react to us simply because we are being honest, indirectly exposing their insecurities. People may joke around by throwing our pain back in our face, simply because they don't want to expose their own. There are those who will still treat us like a victim when we're truly the victor in our story. Then there are our champions, championing us all the way, celebrating us, encouraging us and being free to go on their journey to healing and restoration as well.

Through our courage to be vulnerable, we open the door to deep connection with others and a door to our own healing. I could've become a statistic; another number. I was told that I'd never make it and if I did make it, I'd only repeat the same traumatic cycle. I was told that I'd never amount to anything and that I'd end up as an alcoholic just like my father. I hope that as you read my book, the hardship and traumas I've had to work through to be the free person I am today, will help you or somebody you know to begin their healing journey.

NICOLA RUCCI

PART ONE

My Story

Are you giving the children chocolate?

Chapter 1
DYSFUNCTION BREEDS DYSFUNCTION

"Hardship often prepares an ordinary person for an extraordinary destiny."

C.S. Lewis

I want to start out by saying, I love my mum. We have a very close relationship that took a lot of tears and a lot of talking through all the hurt we had both experienced. Mum shared her side of things with me for many years: she literally went through hell and back. It also gave me a better understanding as to why she did the things she did and said the things she said (especially to me being the eldest child). In all honesty and vulnerability, we grew to love each other very much and my children adore her. Mum is married to a wonderful man called Frank and she has ten grandchildren and two great grandchildren (all who love her). Having said that, life wasn't always this way. I was born into a family of dysfunction: a type of dysfunction that is all too common in our society today.

My Story

My dad was completely dependent on alcohol. He was, in actual fact, an alcoholic. He would come home every night absolutely intoxicated and my mum would just be waiting; never knowing what kind of mood he'd arrive home in. As soon as he entered the front door, my mum would say, "Your dinner is on the table," and she'd wait for his response. Dad wasn't a loving or happy drunk, but irritable and angry; sarcastic, and condescending. There were times when the doctors would say to him over the years, "You will die if you don't stop drinking." But he always said, "I don't have a drinking problem. I'll be perfectly OK" and 'I don't need anyone telling me how to live my life." He constantly vocally denied his drinking and continued to live dependent on the bottle; denying he had a problem. Humility was never one of my father's attributes.

We never celebrated special occasions like Christmas or Easter and sometimes we didn't celebrate birthdays (depending on whose birthday it was). These celebrations were usually ruined because we'd live in the embarrassment of his alcoholic rants. Mum would apologise to us and say, "I'm sorry. It's your father's fault that we aren't giving you a birthday party." She couldn't even begin to organise a birthday, knowing what would take place: more fighting, more arguments and more physical abuse. Besides, what would other people say?

One Friday night, in the middle of winter, my brother David and sister Fiona were huddled with me around a big bar heater in the living room, staying warm while watching TV. I was five years old, David was three, and Fiona just one year old. Suddenly, Dad burst through the front door. He didn't greet us, but simply yelled "Where's my dinner, woman!" Mum was waiting, like she always did. She immediately turned to me and said, "Take your brother and sister into their bedrooms, close the door and don't come out." So I did. That became the normal routine most nights: I'd take my brother and sister into their bedroom, shut the door and wait for the arguments to stop. David, at three years old, would say, "It's time to put our fingers in our ears," in the hope to block out the noise from the pending fight. I'd stay with them in their room and play with the toys, trying to distract them. Once Dad had passed out in his chair, Mum would quickly come into the room and get us ready for bed and I'd wait until they were asleep and then go back to my room. It was routine, so firmly pressed into my memory.

On this winter's night, Mum had his dinner in her hand. When my dad shouted, "Where's my dinner, woman!" she threw it at him. From the bedroom, I heard the plate hit the floor and break into pieces. Mum had had enough. She just couldn't cope anymore with his arrogance and his drunken demands, followed by abuse. Most nights, Mum would run to her bedroom and lock him out. That's when he'd sit high and mighty in his chair yelling out at the top of his voice, "You're stupid! You're the stupidest woman! You're nothing; absolutely nothing!" Those words would keep going on and on, gradually getting quieter, until he passed out. Some nights weren't as bad, but we didn't grow up in a peaceful household. I watched my mum trying very hard to avoid upsetting him, tiptoeing around him in fear of the next angry outburst and carrying tension and anxiety.

My father was never physically abusive to us as children, but he was verbally abusive. He was good at using words to hurt us. He was condescending, sarcastic and demeaning. He'd tell us we weren't good enough and he'd lash out in anger, but he'd never hit us. He'd get so angry and look like he was going to hit us, but we'd cower and then somewhere inside of him, something would tell him that that was enough to get his point across. He was a drinker well before my mother married him, but he became solely dependent on alcohol during the beginning of their marriage. My mother explained to me that she was hoping that he'd change for the better after their marriage and more so with the new responsibility of having children, but sadly that never happened. It just got worse day by day.

My brother, David, and I were born on Thursday Island (which is an island in a group of islands in the Torres Strait, off the tip of Cape Yorke Peninsula in Queensland, Australia). Dad was employed with the Queensland Public Service and was transferred to Thursday Island to work for The Aboriginal and Islander Affairs Department. He was a mathematician and his accounting skills were of the highest level. He also became one of the islands voluntary ambulance drivers and would get called up when the other ambos weren't available. Everyone knew my father on the island — especially the police. But his reputation wasn't always a good one. He'd get so intoxicated, that the police would put him in overnight lock-up and tell my mum to enjoy a peaceful night without him. Mum said that it was a relief when the police would knock on her door to tell her, "Jonny boy is sleeping it off in our cell." His reputation always preceded him but, somehow, he held his public service job and managed a lot of staff in the process. Dad may have had a brilliant mathematical brain and strong work ethic, but he was destroying his family's lives. My mum thought moving to Thursday Island and away from my father's mates who all drank heavily would solve their problems and his drinking would slow down, but the isolation of the island only contributed to his pain and the deep-rooted issues he carried from his childhood. So his drinking escalated. When Mum fell pregnant with my sister Fiona, they decided to come back to Brisbane, where they'd been living before. I was five years old when we arrived in Brisbane and that's when our lives changed for the worse.

My father's childhood was anything but peaceful. My dad's mother passed away when he was seven years old. He had an older brother and two younger siblings. He never overcame the death of his mum. His dad, my granddad, remarried again and 'Grandma' (as I knew her), took on four children that weren't her own. She faced a lot of challenges especially with dad, because he resented her and never got on with her. We didn't visit Granddad and Grandma very often, but when we did, I'd only hear arguing. My grandad would take the kids outside, so we wouldn't hear dad and grandma fighting and while we were waiting for the fighting to stop, Grandad would give us chocolate. He loved his chocolate, and Grandma would tell him off and say, "Jim! Are you giving the children chocolate?" He'd say, "No dear" with a great big smile on his face. He'd hide chocolate all the time from Grandma (he had a secret stash in the garage that only we knew was there!). Grandma was direct. She'd tell you straight and tell you exactly what she thought. This meant, she also told my dad he was an alcoholic (which never went down too well with my father). My grandad would just stay out of it. He was always trying to keep the peace without getting involved, but not my grandma. She always said what had to be said and she didn't care if it offended you or not. Their arguments always ended in someone walking out and that was usually my father. Then it was time to leave without saying goodbye to them again. I often saw my grandfather in the distance looking sadly at my father.

Not long after we arrived back in Brisbane, my mum was put onto a well-known anonymous organisation, that helps families and friends of alcoholics recover from the impact thereof. They gave my mum the time and support she needed at that point, but it was getting too hard to live with Dad. Every night he'd come home drunk and every night she'd be on edge; not knowing what he'd be like when he came through the front door. One day she went to seek a counsellor and was finally referred to a psychologist. After a couple of sessions, she was encouraged to leave him.

She packed her things and left, just before my father got home from work. I watched her packing that day and I said to her, "Where are you going mum?" She stayed silent. I now know she was experiencing a nervous breakdown and couldn't cope with any more of my father's abusive drunken behaviour. But as a child, all I knew was mum didn't take us with her. There was no warning and no goodbye. It was just me, my brother and sister alone with Dad now.

Dad sold the house we lived in and moved to a cheaper suburb and paid for a nanny to come and look after us while he was at work. The nanny's name was Tracey. She was twenty-four years old and had a baby of her own. Tracey would arrive in the mornings with her baby before Dad left for work. Once he left, I'd get ready for school and my brother ready for preschool. Then Tracey would spend the day with my sister and her own baby. I'd walk twenty minutes to school with my brother and drop him off at the preschool attached to the primary school. Then he'd stay there until I finished school, and I'd pick him up and we'd walk home together. The weekends without Tracey were always the worst days for me. We'd be up early on Saturday morning and by midmorning Dad would be right on his way to being drunk. We'd go to the horse races (usually Eagle Farm or the Doomben Racetrack in Brisbane). We'd enter the gates around lunchtime and Dad would go straight to the betting ring to bet on his winners. Afterwards, we'd go and get some lunch (usually hot chips) and would sit waiting for the races to start. I'd look after my brother and sister while Dad would slip away to get a drink. I'd make up games to play so David and Fiona didn't misbehave getting bored while waiting to go home.

I was six years old and at that age I was very aware of other people coming to talk to us, as if they'd never seen kids before at racetracks. But it was uncommon for children to be there. We were usually the only kids there, especially with a drunk parent. I was always trying to protect us from strange people. I remember being asked once by a woman, "Uhm, are you here with anyone?" I went on to say, "Yes, my mother and father will be back in a moment." I'd lie to protect us. I knew the scenario of being at a racetrack with an intoxicated father wasn't normal. However, that was probably the only time anyone ever cared why we were at the races all hours of the day and night.

I remember my brother and I'd find money lying around: money that people had dropped while either being drunk themselves or in between putting a bet on the horses. When this happened, we'd give the money to Dad to make him happy. We were completely aware that Dad's mood was determined by his winnings or his losses. I hated the racing industry – a feeling that still stands to this day. I hated it for its complete waste of money and the way the horses were treated. For some, a day out at the races is wonderful and they have a really great time. For me it was always a horrible Saturday or Saturday night. I saw a lot of angry people lose a lot of money and I saw a lot of drunk people acting in strange and out-of-control ways. My awareness was heightened because of my father.

Dad wasn't just a drinker, but also a huge gambler. He lost thousands of dollars and though he'd also win at times, the losing far outweighed the winning. He never knew when to give up. He'd just keep going even when he lost the lot. He used to say to me "the horses will bring us good luck today." All I remember of luck, was Dad's mood reliant on his winnings or losses that determined entirely how much more he would drink when we arrived back home. My father didn't drive a lot. He lost his license due to his alcohol consumption. So we'd catch public transport. This often added to our embarrassment and humiliation when we tried to get our drunk father into a cab or onto a bus or a train. People always watched but nobody ever said anything.

We'd go to any of the racetracks on weekends: the dog races, the horse races or the harness races which were at night. One night at the harness races, we were waiting for Dad to come out of the betting ring. He was usually the last person to leave, because he wouldn't only grab his winnings if he won, but he'd study the horses to see if he could decide the winner for the next time. So we'd wait, as I held onto my sister and yelled at my brother to come back to where I was. My brother was always running away and I was always chasing after him. This one night, Dad staggered out drunkenly and I immediately told David to hail a taxi. He put his little thumb out so the cab driver would see (he copied other people doing it). The taxi came over and I put Fiona and David into the back seat and helped Dad into the front passenger seat. The taxi driver never said anything. As per usual he'd ask me for our address because Dad couldn't answer.

As I grew older, I never understood why people didn't ask if we were alright – three young children waiting outside the Albion Racetrack at ten o'clock at night and sometimes until a whole lot later. No one ever asked any questions. They simply mumbled under their breath, "Why are those kids outside so late at night?" I think about all those years, doing the same thing most weekends. Nobody took us away, nobody alerted the authorities, nobody kidnapped us.

I learnt how to make my way around Brisbane and especially the northern side of Brisbane, where we lived. Whether it was by bus, train or taxi, I'd learn the street names, the bus routes and the train timeline on the north side. If you told me a street name, I'd know how to get there.

We were always somewhere. If it wasn't the races, it was a pub. Back in the early 70s, a lot of pubs didn't allow children inside so we'd sit outside on the curb, waiting for Dad to finish up. Back then, beer gardens became a thing and we were able to sit outside while he would have his drinks at the table. I felt like I knew every pub in Brisbane – we were always there. Dad always had good luck at winning the meat tray at the pubs, so we'd often go home with a full meat tray that would last us a couple of weeks or until he won the next one. Some Saturday mornings, before the races, we'd end up in the Brisbane CBD and I always remember the newspaper boys calling out their price for the newspapers. It always had a distinct call and so did the smell of the city. I loved being in the city with all its different people rushing to and from wherever they had to be. I watched and observed people and tried to figure out who they were and what type of home life they were living in or trying to create for their family.

I didn't know I carried trauma from my childhood; I just grew up learning to cope the best way I knew how. I became aware of my inner self as I got older and how certain situations and circumstances made me feel. I now know that I carried a lot of internal anxiety. I remember the nervous feelings I would get, nervous to the point of throwing up. The anxiety would rise just before Dad would come home at night. I'd make sure that my brother and sister were settled and Tracey would be in the kitchen getting our dinner ready and as soon as he opened the door, Tracey would get her things, her baby and leave. She knew exactly what he was like. I learnt to shut down my anxiety, so I could be aware of what was going on. David and I'd try and find all the alcohol when dad was passed out either in his chair or in his bed and we'd pour it all down the sink. It worked for a little while, but he'd always find other places to put it. We'd tell him he drank it all the night before. Of course, he never believed us.

I was constantly anticipating Mum's return home. I'd look out my window and watch the cars drive by. I'd look to see if she was out there. I was always waiting and I was always hoping she'd come back. I'd reassure my brother on the way to school, "Mummy will come back – you'll see!" in a positively determined voice and he'd always say, "I know she will, Nikki." I remember his beautiful little smile and the innocence of that smile, never knowing what the days will bring to us, what pain we were going to encounter and who will cause the pain.

There was a night when Mum turned up with Grandma, Dad's step mum. He went into a full rage and told them to leave the property, but I got out. I ran out the front gate and was watching and listening to the argument from outside the front fence, but Fiona and David were still inside. My grandma thought she could coax them out of the house so mum could take us, but Dad was very cunning and he wouldn't let David and Fiona leave. Fiona was distraught, crying and calling out to me, so naturally I went back to her and Mum and Grandma left. He got so drunk that night. All I was waiting for was for him to pass out in that chair of his. That night never happened again. Dad gave Tracey strict instructions to never let my grandma and my mum come inside and take us. But Tracey was a mum herself and I still remember the anguish on her face when Dad said that.

Then it happened. One day I walked home from school with my brother and there she was. Our mum had come back for us, she had packed as many of our things as she could and we said goodbye to Tracey. Meanwhile Dad was at work – not knowing any of this was taking place, even though he'd given Tracey strict instructions not to let us go with Mum. I remember the look on Tracey's face; fearful as she hesitantly said goodbye and let us go. I just know that she knew living with my father was a disaster in the making. I don't know what happened after we left Tracey, but she'd have had a lot of explaining to do when Dad was home from work and I know that wouldn't have gone down too well. Maybe, just maybe, she left before he got home – I will never know. Tracey was a really kind person; she helped bring some kind of order into our life. We had food on the table and we didn't starve. The starvation we endured was that of security, stability and love.

My father had no idea where we were; Mum never told him. By this stage I was seven and a half years old and Mum had been gone a whole fifteen months. There were a couple of times in that period that she'd tried to see us, but Dad wouldn't let her and she didn't want to deal with his aggressive behaviour. But as my brother and I walked home from school, we opened up the front door and found Mum waiting for us. We were so excited! I thought that now that she was back and ready to take us away, everything would be OK and we were going to be safe. We got our things and got into a car with another man who was driving. Nobody said anything in the car, except David and Fiona who was fighting and me telling them to shut up. I was studying the new man who was driving and trying to work out what kind of person he was going to be. In the time Mum was gone, she'd met some new friends, parents who were going through similar circumstances as herself and there she was introduced to this new man; this man driving; this new man who we were going to live with.

We got out of the car and Mum introduced us to him. His name was John, just like my father. He was bald, medium-sized, a Vietnam war veteran; he seemed nice enough. One day, I was looking for something and I came across pornography magazines. In fact, I realised they were everywhere in the house. Out of curiosity, I started to flick through them and I still remember my response to looking at them: I felt physically sick. I was physically sick. I wasn't even nine years old. A child shouldn't be exposed to such images. Yet, I was deeply unaware he was about to rob me of my childhood innocence.

Trauma was interwoven with each stage of my young life.

Chapter 2
THE TAPESTRY OF TRAUMA

"Trauma is the emotional, psychological and physiological residue left over from heightened stress that accompanies experiences of threat, violence, and life-challenging events."

The Australian Childhood Foundation (2019)

I was always OK during the day, but it was at night when I felt the anxiety rise and I'd get nervous. I began to leave a light on at night. There were a lot of other hidden emotions being buried layer upon layer of trauma that was taking place in our lives. I call it the Tapestry of Trauma, because my trauma was interwoven with each stage of my young life.

John had a filthy depraved mind. He started to open my bedroom door at night and come over to my bed. He started to molest my tiny body, touching me in places that no child should ever experience. Mum would be asleep and wouldn't have any idea of what was going on. I remember one night I said, "Go away and leave me alone!" He did for a little while and the door wouldn't open and I thought I was safe from that happening again. But it wasn't long before he started to come into my room again late at night, this time more aggressively. It was as if he wanted to make the point clear; that he was in control. I often didn't sleep through the night simply because I never knew what was going to happen, the fear of what he would do kept me awake.

John always said to me that it was our secret. Isn't that always the child molester's way? I'd experienced a lot already in my short life, but even so, I'd no idea what to do with a man like John and no one had ever touched me like he did. I knew how to fight, I knew how to protect David and Fiona, but no one had taught me to fight for myself. I had no idea how to tell someone what was happening or if I even could tell someone what was happening.

David witnessed it one night; he saw what John was doing to me. We were living in a two-bedroom house at the time, so we all had to sleep in the same bedroom. I call it the house of horrors, because in this house was more turmoil than in all my young life put together. My brother and sister were in bunk beds and I had my own bed on the other side of the room. John was so brazen. He came into our bedroom thinking that we were all asleep. I remember the face I pulled pushing him to go away. I didn't know David was still awake, but he saw everything John did to me that night. My brother kept it to himself for years and years.

John also began to physically beat my mum. It happened during arguments over the most mundane things. What helped were the weekends at Dad's place. We eventually went to see Dad on weekends, because mum and dad got divorced and the courts awarded him weekends with us. Going to Dad's, believe it or not, was an escape, because it was time away from John. It felt like the lesser of the two evils. I'd say to myself, "It's OK Nikki, it's not as bad as being with John." I learnt to know what to expect with Dad, but John was now the unpredictable one. Mum would drop us off to Dad on Friday nights and she'd pick us up on Sunday nights and it was my responsibility to make sure my siblings were safe during those 48 hours. I had a system and routine with Dad; I knew how to get from one place to another when Dad took us to the racetracks or the pubs. I knew how to look after David and Fiona. I had some street smarts about me because that is where we'd end up most weekend nights – on the streets waiting outside the racetrack for Dad. When we got home from being out all day, I'd get my brother and sister into their pyjamas and then get them into bed. Some nights were hard because they wouldn't listen to me and they just exhausted me. Eventually I'd go to bed while Dad slept in his chair all night. This was routine, every weekend.

When I was eleven years old, I found the courage to tell Dad that John was hurting us, but I didn't tell him that John was sexually abusing me. I was just testing Dad to see what he'd do. John often beat David black and blue too, so that was enough for Dad to confront John. My father wasn't a very big man, so confronting John one night didn't work because John was much bigger and stronger, so he just punched him in the face and he fell to the ground, breaking his glasses and leaving a black eye. What didn't help is Dad always drinking and often picked fights while intoxicated. Like in the pub, he would always come off second best, with a black eye or a broken nose, or some broken ribs, which we would often experience watching and often screaming, telling whoever was beating him up to let him go. It only further added to my feelings of insecurity and lack of stability.

I didn't tell mum what John was doing to me either. I was scared to tell her. I thought she'd perhaps challenge him and I knew this was unsafe – John would beat her up leaving deep bruises and broken bones in her body. He was an extremely violent man and he was strong and so these secrets just became a normal part of our life. Mum would often say, "Don't tell anyone what is going on," so we never told anyone. However, this one Saturday afternoon, Mum and John got into yet another argument and I heard screaming from the bedroom. Mum had run behind the bedroom door, John opened the door and slammed it on her face, this time breaking her jaw and her rib cage. I immediately took my brother and sister outside into the backyard to get away from what was happening. All I could think about doing was keeping us safe. Our next-door neighbour at the time heard the screaming and knocked on the door. She came inside and saw the state my mother was in and helped Mum get to the hospital. John took off in his car and while mum was being taken to hospital, we waited for our next-door neighbour to come back and look after us, while mum was gone. The doctor wired her jaw up and the police gave my mother a contact for a women's shelter. After being abused for years by John and watching him beat up Mum and especially my brother over anything, we left to go to the women's shelter. Finally, a safe place. I will be forever grateful to our next-door neighbour for being caring towards us that day.

The women's shelter we moved to, was an old Catholic Convent. It had big dormitory style rooms with several beds in each dormitory. It had big white walls and we each had a bed. It felt cold and uninviting, but the beautiful nuns (also called "sisters") were warm and loving and gave us a safe place to live for six months. They counselled us and talked to the police about putting a restraining order out against John. They taught my mother how to budget to the last cent we had, giving her the confidence to rent her own home without the help of anyone. This was lifesaving for Mum because she no longer felt she had to rely on someone else's income to give us a roof over our heads, which she would often say she needed. We didn't have to stay in unsafe situations anymore.

There was a huge fountain in the courtyard of the women's shelter and I was sitting around it when one of the nuns came to me and asked me how I was doing. I was only twelve years old. I felt safe to open up to her about John. I remember her calm voice and she just oozed a warm comforting feeling; it was the first time I actually felt I was really loved and it was the first time I heard about Jesus and His love for me.

Because I felt that safety when speaking with the nun, I decided to tell mum what John had been doing to me. She was horrified – but not with John. Her response was, "You are a dirty little girl for allowing that to happen." I remember yelling at her and saying, "It started when I was seven and a half. How could I have stopped him? He always beat you up. What was I supposed to do?"

As a child, I always felt like I was the problem and that it was my fault that my mum left, that my parents divorced, that I was the reason we had to leave John and that I was the one who made life so hard. When she told me I was dirty and expressed that I allowed sexual abuse to happen to me, those words only made me feel shameful and guilty. It also made me feel ugly, condemned and worthless. As adults, Mum and I have spoken a lot about those early years. She does recall what she said to me (calling me a dirty little girl), but she can't recall why she said it or why she blamed me. My mum was going through a lot internally, let alone physically. Telling her about John was just one more layer of guilt to carry. Therefore, instead of carrying the guilt herself and doing something proactive about the abuse, she passed the blame and guilt onto me. Mum's emotional capacity was eroded. I didn't see that or understand that when I was young. I closed up, never to mention it again.

I will be forever grateful for the incredible nuns, who helped us with our trauma. They helped my mother with her confidence and got us back on our feet. We lived somewhere in the Ashgrove area and Mum landed a job with a Brisbane newspaper company and eventually became the secretary to the editor of that company. We went back to the school we'd been to a few years earlier.

I really struggled with school. I went to eleven schools. I hated having to walk through a new set of gates at a new school; the smell and uncertainty of who the children would be in my classroom. But I remember this one school: I'd be at the fence screaming my lungs out at Mum, saying, "I don't want to be here!" I was fearful; fearful of being pushed away by other kids who didn't know me. I was fearful of what the new teacher was like, because not all teachers were warm and understanding of the situation we lived in. I could tell which teachers loved to teach and which teachers really hated it. Some teachers would concentrate on the smart kids and leave the students who struggled to learn and figure it out on their own. Then, there were the teachers who loved the students who struggled to learn and such teachers were meant to be teachers.

I used to sit by myself a lot in the lunchtime breaks and I started enjoying it. I'd watch and observe the other children playing with each other and sometimes I was asked if I wanted to join when they were playing their skipping rope games. Some schools I attended had remedial classes and others didn't. One of the things I could do was spell words and read singular words. I'd win the spelling bee contests at school, but I couldn't read two sentences after one another. Even though I had trouble writing the words down and reading sentences, I was good at spelling the words out loud, which instilled some confidence within me. Back in the 1970s, teachers taught number facts by rhythm and song – a brilliant way for children to remember them. So, I'd sing my number facts to myself every day. I did however flourish in art class. It didn't matter what art we were doing, I just loved it and I was good at it. Art was my escape from the realities of my home life. Most kids like art, but for me it helped me to forget about what was going on at home. I loved to draw, paint and copy any of the famous painters' work like Vincent Van Gogh. I also enjoyed athletics. When I realised I was good at it, I became very competitive in order to show people I was good at something. I loved to run and play sport. I enjoyed anything sporty: netball, touch footy (if it involved being outside of the classroom, I was there). I felt safe outdoors where people could see me, because nothing bad happened to me when I was outside surrounded by other people.

Mum had to be at work early and she wouldn't get home until 6pm every weeknight. Because I liked systems and routine, it wasn't long before I set myself up in one. That's how I coped. Everything that had to be done – washing the clothes, hanging it out, doing the dishes, making the beds, doing my homework, helping my brother do his and then helping my sister with hers – had a timeline that I had set up and it had to be done by the time she got home. I'd make sure I helped with the dinner or part of the dinner, so she wasn't stressed. I was always trying to alleviate stress in the home. Whether it was with Mum or at Dad's – I'd always try to help.

One day, Mum had to go to hospital. It was a day surgery operation: she was gone early in the morning and came home at night. For a couple of weeks, she couldn't do a lot. Therefore, it was up to me to look after my brother and sister and keep the home going. I was used to doing that anyway. So, at twelve years old, it was an easy thing to do. But on this particular day, we were walking home from school, and I saw out of the corner of my eye someone driving very slowly up the road. I looked over and I noticed it was John. He was watching us walk, looking over at us and was trying to get our attention. Somehow, he found out where we were going to school and waited for us to come out of the school gates and followed us from there. I told my brother and sister sternly, "Don't run into the block of units we're living in. John is following us." David yelled and said, "I hate that man!" Fiona held my hand tightly. My heart was racing and I had to think quickly. I said, "Let's walk up to the corner where the Anglican Church is and see if someone can help us." There was a dance studio there and a dance class had started. So, we walked in. One of the mothers of the students came towards us seeing the terrified look on our faces. She asked us whether we were OK. I pointed to the car John was driving as I told her what was going on. He had stopped at a red traffic light right opposite the church and she was able to copy down his number plate. She went back inside the studio to call the police. The police told her that he had a restraining order against him. That was the very last time we saw John. I'll never forget that lady. I'm forever grateful that someone took the time to care about us that day. John tried to come back into my mother's life multiple times, manipulating his way back in and often succeeding, but this time he was unsuccessful. He never tried again – four years of his torment and brutality was over.

I thank God for the church up at the end of Jubilee Terrace on a main road. It was there for everyone to see; not in a back street somewhere out of sight. It was open and not closed. There were people there ready to help, even though I was anxious. I felt safe the moment we walked into the dance class. The lady that helped us that day will never know the impact she had on three young children. She stopped something from happening to us that could've completely destroyed us. She went out of her way to protect us from a predator. She could've turned a blind eye and told us to leave, but she didn't; she protected us. I'll always be grateful to her.

After Mum healed from surgery, we moved out of the apartment and into a house. I was thirteen years old and in grade eight by now and Mum had met another man whom she married. His name was Don and Don was also a drinker. He wasn't as bad as my father, but still the same kind of behaviours started taking place. It was a cycle with Mum – she needed to be needed. She needed a man in her life, but she would always find the most broken men and would bring them home. Don was just as broken as the other men that came before him. Somewhere in my mother's psyche, she thought she didn't deserve to be loved. That was a lie she'd believed. In fact, quite the opposite was true: she did deserve to be loved and highly valued.-

Don had a boat and he taught us how to water ski. We'd go to Stradbroke Island on the weekends when we weren't with Dad. Those weekends at Stradbroke Island were great. We'd help put the tent up and then go and find seashells on the beach. I loved the smell of the ocean and the sand between my toes. I loved being in the ocean. I loved the feeling of being sunburnt too. There's nothing like having a sunburnt body after a great time at the beach! As I got older, I got tougher with Mum. John was gone for good, but she had Don now. I'd say, "I'm not going to see Father anymore." But she needed me to look after my brother and sister. Dad would get angry if I didn't turn up, so I couldn't get out of not seeing him. Dad moved around a lot in Brisbane. His job in the public service took him all over Queensland as a relieving hospital manager. He'd manage the hospitals out in the West (in the country areas for periods of three to six months), when the employees went on holiday or resigned. He'd then fill the position. When he went out to those country towns, it gave me a break from seeing him on the weekends. It also gave me a break from always being consciously aware of where my brother and sister were. They got up to so much mischief and would run up and down the streets hiding from me while Dad was in his drunken state.

My brother was a naughty kid. He'd go down to the train station and get on and off trains trying to run away from the train conductors and I was always chasing him home. When I finally got him, the train conductors would call us "little delinquents"; never trying to understand and help us in our circumstances. We weren't their problem of course. This was all outcomes of our extremely dysfunctional home life.

Don's adult children lived in Townsville. They invited us there and said, "Why don't you all come and live here?" So, we packed everything up and went to live in Townsville. I remember the feeling of loss again – my anxiety would come flooding back like dark clouds rolling in for a storm to hit. It was due to the fear of the unknown and that fear inside of me was very real. I loved living in Brisbane because I knew Brisbane. I knew the surrounding suburbs where we lived like a map on the palm of my hand. We walked the city streets throughout the weekends. But I didn't know Townsville. Another set of school gates needed to be walked through; new school mates were awaiting – it was happening all over again. Those nervous sick feelings that I always felt, were coming again every time we moved. I got nervous and I'd always try to shut those emotions out. But it got harder as I got older. So, I'd pour myself into my artwork and my running and got involved in sports. I always said to myself that I'd never become like my father.

After I finished my ninth year at Newmarket State High School in Brisbane, I started my tenth year at Townsville State High School in North Queensland. Don's drinking got worse. He never touched me, but I always felt him looking at me. That's why I put a towel over the keyhole of my bedroom to make sure he wasn't looking into that keyhole (which I always felt him doing). He liked looking up women's dresses and going for his beach walks along the nude beaches. He always told me how beautiful I was (which was creepy). I always made sure I wore shorts or jeans. He was a pervert and a manipulator. He'd look at you with a sad expression to get you to do something for him. Mum just shrugged it off as if it was nothing to worry about – after all, he wasn't as bad as John. Nobody ever spoke up. It was like a silent conversation that wasn't allowed to be spoken of. This cycle was on repeat and somewhere, somehow, I didn't want this same cycle to be a part of my future self.

After five years of marriage to Don, I finally persuaded my mum to leave him this time. I was determined to tell her not to put up with him hitting her and him always being drunk. I was seventeen and feisty and would tell Don to his face to stop hurting Mum. I had a fight in me that said, "That's it! Enough is enough." With the divorce settlement from Don's house, Mum was able to buy her own two-bedroom unit to live in. I was entering grade twelve at this stage and eventually graduated. I applied for a job at the defence forces with the Australian Air Force. I passed all my exams and was offered a job as a Signals Officer, but with Mum's divorce, I decided to defer my employment for twelve months. It also gave me time to figure out if it was something that I really wanted to do. Twelve months to the day I was contacted by them and I told them that I'd decided not to join. I ended up applying for a job at the Townsville general hospital working in medical records and setting appointments with patients. It was an entry administration job, checking in patients for their clinic appointments and setting new appointments for them.

A big part of breaking the cycle was my determination to finish school. I worked extremely hard in the last two years of high school. My sister had dropped out of school and didn't graduate from grade ten and my brother only went to grade nine. To his credit, his dyslexia was worse than mine; he struggled to read or write. Even with the remedial classes he had, he didn't want to learn. But I was determined to learn and get some schooling behind me.

I learnt to read better and started writing more fluently. I remember how my grade ten English teacher at Townsville State High encouraged me in my reading and writing to the point where I passed my English exams for the first time in my schooling years. My English teacher made a massive impact on my life. He was a standout teacher that loved his job and would go the extra mile to help his students excel. He didn't only focus on the bright kids in the class. One of the teachers in my second year at school helped me feel secure; she knew my home life was in turmoil. I thank these teachers for taking the time to notice me and who helped me grow.

Trauma remembers its origin and our traumatic responses to such trauma can be passed down from one generation to another. As I've said, my dad had childhood trauma growing up – losing his mother was a traumatic experience for him. Seeing his father go through the grieving process made Dad grieve more. He didn't like seeing his father cry. He resented his new mother and would tell her so; cementing firmly the hurt and hatred and never dealing with the pain. Eventually he tried to drown his pain in alcohol that resulted in irreversible damage to our family. Dad never married again after the divorce. There was never any other woman in his life. He remained single for the rest of his life.

My mum, on the other hand, grew up in a secure family environment. My grandfather, who was a professed atheist and a very loving man, served in England as an RAF fighter pilot during World War II. He had enough of war, fighting and arguments to last the rest of his life. When the war ended, he went to Cambridge University and obtained a degree in high school education. During the war however, when my grandmother was pregnant again, she asked my great aunty Phyllis if she'd take my mother to live with her. My grandmother wasn't coping with two children and an additional number three on the way. The war made life feel so unpredictable and unsafe. That's why my mum went to live with my great aunty Phyllis for over five years. Aunty Phyllis couldn't have children of her own. She'd lost her first husband in WWI and her second in WWII. She was alone in her big house and had a lot of love to give to my mum.

One day my grandmother knocked on aunty Phyllis' door and asked for my mother back. They'd bought ten-pound tickets for a ship that was on its way to Australia. To this day, my mum says that she was closer to her aunty Phyllis than her biological mother and the trauma and rejection of having to leave her aunty whom she loved so much, would later show itself in a crisis.

My grandmother was a strong woman. She wasn't always affectionate, but still created that homely feeling. She became a nurse and graduated as a matron. She had a reputation in the medical profession of being a "hard matron." Nurses and doctors feared her. She was a perfectionist and meticulous in her field of work.

Everything needed to be done correctly and perfectly. She kept everyone in line and on their toes. My mum would often say that when they were growing up, they'd never have a sick day off school; Grandma would know whether they were truly sick or not. The family moved to Australia when Mum was fifteen years old; it was a huge and personal move for her. At this time, Mum was very naive about abuse of any kind. She'd never experienced abuse. My grandparents would never disagree or argue about any issues in front of Mum or her siblings. They always made sure to argue in private, so the kids never listened to what was going on. So how was Mum to know that arguments were a normal feature of any relationship and then resolving those disagreements? My grandparents failed to normalise disagreements and teach their children any sort of conflict management or resolution.

Mum rarely got any support from her own parents, so she always looked for support in other places: other places that ended up physically and emotionally abusing her. She carried her own scars. She was beaten by her partners. She was emotionally and verbally abused. She experienced trauma to the point of emotional breakdown. She was, in actual fact, a victim of domestic violence. And that wasn't OK.

NICOLA RUCCI

Chapter 3
GARY

When I was sixteen and in my eleventh year at school, my friend wanted to go dancing in a night club. I went along to see what the fuss was all about. In 1983, it was common practice to let all the girls in without an ID regardless of how old they were. We were usually around sixteen and seventeen (still in high school) and most of us just wanted to dance. The girls would bring the guys and the guys usually had more money to spend. So, the bouncers at the door would let us in.

This one particular night, there was a group of young men a little older than us sitting at a table not too far away from ours. I was aware of who they were but really didn't take much notice, because my friend was getting very drunk. Not being much of a drinker myself, I was naturally keeping an eye on her. After a little while, I told my friend that we should leave and go home; simply because, by this stage, she was slurring her words, not making sense and throwing up (Keep in mind what I experienced with my father and Don: I automatically went into "mother mode" and wanted to get home safely). Just as I said, "Let's go home," the young men at the table replied, "There's a party going on! Who wants to come?" My friend wasn't going home at all: We were going to the party! Why did I want to go to this party? Well, I didn't. I was looking out for my friend. So, we all got into the back of this Ute and went to the party. The person driving was my now husband, Gary. When we got to the party, all I could see were drugs and alcohol and everyone either getting stoned or drunk. It wasn't the place I wanted to be. I'd made up my mind when I was a young girl that I never wanted to get married, to have children and be a part of drugs and alcohol. Being at this party was going against everything I'd made up my mind about. I had a plan and I wasn't going to change that plan. As I was looking around for someone to take me home, I walked into the kitchen and saw Gary standing there. Out of all the people at this party, he wasn't drunk. He knew he had to drive his Ute home, so I thought: He must be a responsible person to have that frame of mind in this atmosphere. I went straight up to him and asked him whether he'd take my friend and I home and he agreed. As I got into his Ute, he said to me, "You aren't like the other girls. You seem different." That was the start of a friendship with him that would eventually turn into a lifelong marriage.

He asked me out on my very first date. I was seventeen. I didn't own a dress because I always wore shorts or jeans. I had a part time job on weekends at a service station, putting fuel in people's cars and checking under the bonnet to see if they needed oil and water in the radiator. I was a good saver of my money, so I went to a really nice shop and bought myself my first dress. I remember trying on so many dresses feeling uncomfortable every time I put one on. But nonetheless, I bought one and wore it on my first date. Gary picked me up and we went to "The Mandarin Palace" – a Chinese restaurant. We were both very nervous making conversations about nothing and everything. I smile at those early years; they were very precious. After we finished dinner, we went for a walk along the beach called, "The Strand" in Townsville. Afterwards, he drove me back home.

I took our friendship very slow and right from the start I told him that I was never getting married or having children. I thought to myself: he needs to know from the start if this friendship was going to go any further. With Gary, I saw a young man that had vision for his life, a young man that took responsibility for his life to be someone. He asked me why I was adamant I wouldn't get married or have children, so I told him about the abuse that took place when I was young. It was more of a test than anything. I was testing him to see how he would respond to me. He just listened and he also wanted to find John and make him pay for doing what he did to me. I knew then that I'd made the right decision. But not everyone would respond like Gary; not everyone was like him. I was still in high school and Gary had just finished his apprenticeship as a painter and decorator.

He went to work for another painting company, that often had staff dinners and celebrations.

I was invited along to his company's staff barbecue. It was a great night with lots of laughs and a real sense of family — something that I'd never before experienced. When everyone had left, we were asked to stay back to have a cup of tea and some leftover cake. We were having a great conversation about how things were going with me in my eleventh year and what I wanted to do when I finished school. Then, right out of the blue, the boss' wife started sharing with us her faith journey with God. Gary's boss wasn't a Christian and apologised to us for his wife's brazenness. But we said, "It's very interesting." She kept going. I remember sitting there and listening to her story of miracles and healing and how much God loves us; that He loved us enough to die on a cross for us to be free from all our hurts, sicknesses and sin. Boy, she didn't leave any stone unturned! She got straight to the point of salvation. Just before we left, she invited us to go with her and her three gorgeous little girls to church the following Sunday. So we thought, OK! Let's give one Sunday morning in a church service a go. That next Sunday morning was going to change our lives forever.

This love that our friend was telling us about was a love that I first heard at the age of twelve from one of the nuns at the women's shelter and again from a priest in a church we attended once with grandma and grandad during our holiday with them at the beach. I didn't believe in this love and it was hard for me to understand this type of love that came without conditions; a love that overcame, no matter how many mistakes I'd made or how many people I hurt or how many people hurt me or did wrong by me. This was an unconditional love from a God that was so much bigger than me and my circumstances and who was for everyone: I struggled to comprehend such a love.

I didn't grow up going to church every Sunday like most other people. My father was raised Catholic but didn't practice his faith by going to church regularly until he was in his older years. When we were young, he'd take us to a Good Friday Easter service or a midnight mass service at Christmas time, depending on when he'd have us over for those weekends. It wasn't something we did every year because he didn't go every year. However, I do remember the few times we went. My father used the scriptures to instil fear in us. He'd use those same scriptures to hurt Mum. So, going to church was something I never wanted to do. After all, my father wasn't a good example of living out those scriptures anyway. If God was a loving God, then why was my father the opposite?

I remember thinking about the scriptures in the Bible and feeling conflicted. I'd say, "If God was so loving and gave me my free will to be a Christian or to live a life without faith, then why does Dad demand that we obey the commandments?" I began to feel that I really needed this love from God more than anything in the world. Why? Because I hadn't experienced any love during my youth. I hadn't experienced a love that was consistent and worth putting any sort of confidence in. I wanted to know what it was like to be a Christian; to be someone that felt love and truly believed in it. I wanted to see that my ultimate hope of not becoming like my dad, would come to fruition.

We walked through the doors of this great big auditorium. There was a buzz in the air, lots of laughter, people having conversations and an incredibly friendly person at the door welcoming us in. As we kept walking in, I noticed so many friendly warm people that stopped us and greeted us. They didn't ignore us but included us. Our friend got us a seat and we sat together waiting for the church service to begin. In the meantime, her little girls went to a Sunday school programme. I don't know what we were expecting to see and hear at this church but so far it seemed genuine enough.

After we went to church with our friend, we went away thinking that it was something we were prepared to think about. We left it for a month. Then one Sunday we decided to go again to see whether it was still as friendly as it was the first time. Indeed, it was! That day we decided together to make "going to church" a part of our lives and we became Christians.

It was 2 years later on the 7 June 1986, Gary and I got married. I was nineteen and Gary was twenty-one.

In the early years of my marriage, I'd experience flashbacks of John touching me. It was a big struggle for us. I didn't like Gary looking at my nakedness. I'd cover myself up all the time. The shame I carried really impacted our first year of marriage. Especially what John did to me. Those flashbacks tried to destroy my marriage, but I was determined not to let that happen. I never felt good enough. I never felt I could give Gary all that he needed from me. I'd often say, "You deserve someone better than me. You deserve to be loved by someone else." He'd just hold me and love me even though he had his own traumas to work through. It seems that men experience that extra layer of societal pressure to be harder and tougher. They don't share easily. It takes a lot for a man to open up. But that can change if they're willing to go on their own healing journey.

We walked the journey together. We would pray together, read together, stay positive and believe the words in the Bible. God was the centre of our marriage. From the very beginning, we worked hard to work it out with God and friendships. We'd sharpen each other as iron sharpens iron. But isn't that what marriage is? It's a partnership, a coupling of two people who love each other enough to work through life together. We worked at being equals. I didn't and don't think Gary is better than me and I know he doesn't think that either. We've always been in this together and I knew Gary would be by my side no matter how long the healing journey would take. Gary and I cultivated the word "Sorry" in our home. We'd make each other accountable. If we said or did something wrong, it took both of us to come into agreement. Our marriage has never been one-sided, it has always been "Us" and "We" and "Together," not "I' and "Me" or "My." We had to work at it. It took hard work and a lot of arguments, but we were willing to put in the time and effort.

As time went by, we both had a desire to work with young people. We entered ministry life in our early adult years.

I learned to give myself permission to grieve and to heal. over time.

Chapter 4
HOPE THROUGH GRIEF: ONE DAY AT A TIME

"Grief never ends, but it changes. It's a passage; not a place to stay. Grief isn't a sign of weakness, nor a lack of faith. It's the price of love."

Queen Elizabeth I

My Brother

When David was fourteen and living out west in Cloncurry with our father, an opportunity came up for him to move to Toowoomba to start an apprenticeship as a Jockey. He had a love for horses. When we were growing up going to the racetracks, he would stand there at the fence of the track and say that he wanted to ride the horses like the jockeys we saw. When he got the job as an apprentice he had to go and live with the family who was teaching him all about the racing industry and how to ride those big, beautiful horses. This meant he'd have to wake up 4am sharp and learn disciplines which he never learned growing up. He had a fight in his spirit that always said, "I won't give up." He'd say, "I'm going to be someone when I grow up." Always challenging himself, he was determined to not be like Dad. The family he lived with during his four years of training to be a jockey also brought out his competitive nature and the determination he was going to need to succeed in life. David became one of the leading Jockeys in Queensland. I thank God for the Denman family.

On 14 July 1996, David got on his horse at the Clifford Park races and rode in his last race. Losing my brother seemed like the final straw after everything we'd gone through as children. It was a pain I'd never experienced before. I remember saying to God, "Why my brother? Why now?" I had only just got off the phone to him that very day, laughing at our strange family and him telling me that I'd changed a lot; then saying how good the change in me was. I shared with him my faith, and I shared my hope for my future — our future. David responded, "I can see that by hearing your love for me, but I'm not ready yet for that change in my life." Then he left to prepare for his race. I told him I loved him. Those were our final words.

David would always say to us, "Don't call me on race days because I need to focus and concentrate on preparing for my races." So, we didn't usually call him on those race days. But that Saturday, without me knowing, Mum and her new husband Frank went to Toowoomba to see him. It was a spontaneous decision and it also gave them the opportunity to see Mum's grandchild who was three years old. David's wife was pregnant again with their second child. At the same time Mum was visiting them in Toowoomba, I was sitting at home in Adelaide, thinking of calling David to see how he was doing. But in the back of my mind I thought, "David did tell us not to contact him on race days." I'd just put my two children to bed for an afternoon nap and had the urgent feeling to call him. When I called, David's wife answered the phone and said, "Oh! Your mum is here to see us. It's a family affair today. We don't usually get any calls or visitors because it's race day."

That night, after Gary and I got home from a church youth meeting, I saw that our phone answering machine had three messages on it. I'll never forget those three messages. The first one was from Dad. He was drunk and trying to explain something that had happened to David. I couldn't for the life of me make sense of his words because they were mumbled — he was drunk. Then the next message was Frank. He asked me to call because it was an emergency. Then the last message was from Mum. She said, "Nikki, David has been in a racing accident. He's about to go in a helicopter to the Royal Brisbane hospital from Toowoomba." So, I called immediately and she said that at that point, they were still waiting for the helicopter to land at the Royal Brisbane Hospital. I asked what had happened, but she couldn't give me anything other than they'd put David into an induced coma with possible head injuries.

That night, we put our children to bed and Gary and I slept in the living room waiting for the phone to call. My goodness, did we pray hard that night! I had a distant feeling that David wasn't going to make it. We got another call that night to say he was in surgery. My heart was so heavy. I didn't sleep at all. All I did was pray through the night, hoping he'd come out of surgery with a good report. But again, something was telling me he wasn't going to make it. I prayed, I believed, I trusted, but I still just had this feeling.

That morning we got another call from Frank to say that the surgeon and medical team did everything they could but there was nothing more they could've done to save him. David's head injuries were so bad, that when the surgeon opened him up, he said his brain had extensive damage and they couldn't do anything to bring him back with quality of life. If they tried, he'd end up in a vegetative state for the rest of his life. That is the one thing my brother never wanted. He'd seen so many horrors from the racing industry – his friends in wheelchairs, his friends incapacitated. He never wanted to end up in that state. They put David on life support, allowing him to stay alive so that the family could come to say goodbye to him.

At this stage, I was still in Adelaide, trying to figure out the cheapest flights and the quickest time that I could get to him. We didn't have much money; we couldn't just fork out for an interstate flight. Then, someone in our church at the time kindly paid for my airfare from Adelaide to Brisbane. I arrived at the hospital that day just as they were taking David off life support, a decision that had to be made from his wife. Before I got there, we asked a friend of ours, a pastor in Brisbane, if he could go to the hospital and pray for David. And he did. I will forever be grateful to him for doing that in our hour of need.

I truly believe that somewhere inside of me, I knew he was going to die. I felt like God was preparing me for his death. Two weeks before my brother had the racing accident, I had a dream about somebody dying. I thought it was about my father. In my dream, all the family members were crying. The only person I couldn't see was my father. I remember waking up feeling emotionally worn out like I'd been in a fight with someone. But I know now that it was a dream. I was fighting for it not to happen. It was one of those dreams that you keep thinking about and keeps lingering for days. Before boarding the plane, I asked Mum over the phone how everyone was doing. She responded, "We're all walking and sitting in anticipation of what the outcome will be. One of the family members is rocking to and fro with her legs folded up in her arms on a chair and crying." When Mum told me that, I said, "I saw that image in a dream I had two weeks ago." Then the dream played out when I got to the Royal Brisbane Hospital. The dream was preparing me for what I was going to go through: a lot of pain and heartache.

I walked through the hospital doors and the first person I saw was my brother's wife. Her eyes were so red from crying. As soon as she saw me, she burst out crying again. The grief in her eyes was so painful to see. She took me into his room, and I walked slowly up to David and started talking to him as if he was OK. I didn't want to face the reality that he was dying. I just wanted him to wake up, open his eyes and say, "Hey, let's go home." And everything would be as it was before this happened.

The doctor told me that he could still hear but couldn't respond. The last senses to go are our touch and our hearing. That's the stage David was at just before he died. It was as if he was waiting for me to arrive before he said his last goodbye. They took him off life support and he naturally passed away later that day. I took his hand and it was still warm. I kept speaking to him, "Come on David. Wake up and let's go home." I told him I loved him. I didn't want to go. I just wanted to sit with him and keep talking to him. I didn't want to even accept the fact that this was the end of his life. It wasn't even a pending thought in my mind while I sat with him. Then, the dreaded words came, "He's passed away." I said, "No, no! He's still there. He can't be gone yet." Then I got a very gentle nudge with the words, "Nikki, let's let the nurses look after him now." That day, everything happened in slow motion. I remember seeing what everyone was going through. Mum couldn't stop crying. She was trying to be strong but, in the end, she just let it out. Frank was holding onto her and Dad was still in Toowoomba. He didn't come to the hospital because he was drunk as usual.

The news headlines about Jockey, David 'Flash' Wilkes, were everywhere. I couldn't escape the pain of my loss. His face was on the news, his face was in the newspapers, he was talked about in the streets of Toowoomba. I went into a corner store and the man behind the counter was telling the lady he was serving how very sad the racing accident was. I just stood there listening while my eyes flooded up with tears. People everywhere sent their condolences and as kind gestured as they were, it was all so painful. Earlier on the same day that David had his fall, another young up and coming twenty-four-year-old female Jockey was fatally injured at the nearby Warwick races. These dates, the thirteenth of July and fourteenth of July 1996, will forever be etched into the minds of those who loved them immensely.

Where do I begin to even start talking about the pain I was feeling? The pain was so deep and it felt like it was never going to end. Understanding the stages of grief, helped me to understand my responses to my loss and the responses others had around me. There are no right or wrong ways to grieve through loss and there's no timeline. We are all made so differently and uniquely from one another: grief is very personal and affects every part of our emotional, mental and physical wellbeing.

Very Well Mind (2023) describes the stages of grief as posed by Dr Kubler-Ross. Originally proposed were the five stages of grief. Yet later it was suggested that there are actually seven stages. There's no order to them and I understand them as the following: (1) shock, (2) denial and disbelief, (3) anger and frustration, (4) bargaining, (5) testing the new circumstances (6) depression and intense sadness and (7) integration and acceptance. These stages of grief can also overlap into many areas of our trauma, like unforgiveness, rejection, shame or abuse.

For me personally, shock and denial were the first responses to the loss of my brother. It was a defence mechanism and it was helping me buffer the immediate shock of such a painful event. I quite frankly didn't want to believe he'd died. I wanted him to get up and walk out of the hospital and go back to his racing and live a normal life. It was my immediate reaction to his sudden death. I'd just spoken to him that very day before he had his race, so I couldn't possibly believe his life was over. I was in shock and I literally felt numb to the effect of his loss. However, this was giving my mind time to catch up and process the loss of my brother: it's OK to feel that throughout your time of grief.

As the coffin was being lowered into the ground at the funeral, I saw Mum holding onto Frank and I saw my father shaking uncontrollably. The lowering of the coffin is a finality: he was never coming home again. It was the most horrible pain; a pain I have never felt. I was sitting next to Dad. Fiona, my sister, was sitting next to Mum. For the first time in my life, I felt so helpless and sorry for my father: he was so sick mentally, emotionally and physically. I honestly felt for him. I took his hand as we watched the coffin go. He lost his only son. He absolutely loved David – he was his pride and joy. When my brother went out to Cloncurry, he once again tried to save Dad from himself by doing all the things we always did with the alcohol – throwing it down the sink.

"Pain from loss is often redirected and expressed as anger" - Dr Elizabeth Kubler Ross

Being angry is also a normal response: my mum was angry. Her anger led her to question, "Why was this happening? What did I ever do in my life to deserve this?" The pain is the reason for the anger and it eventually provides us perspective for our loss.

My brother and sister didn't have a good relationship so naturally she was experiencing the regret of never getting to know who her brother really was. That would eat away at her. Nobody can prepare you for the sudden death of a loved one, whether they are family members, a friend or even a beloved pet. We'd been through hell and back as kids. His death was such a shock and it didn't feel real. When I got up to give the eulogy at his funeral and I was standing there in that moment, I thought to myself, "I can't believe I'm standing up here speaking about my own little brother." I felt like I was speaking about someone else's son, brother and husband. I felt like I was in the third person saying the words I was saying. However, I put on a brave face in front of all the people because I just wanted it to be over. The Toowoomba racing industry was at his funeral and there were well over 2000 people giving their condolences to us as a family as the media was filming the funeral from outside the church. I just wanted the day to end. I didn't want the cameras filming my brother's funeral. I wanted him alive and I wanted this to be over.

In the bargaining stage of grief we go through a time of wanting to do anything and sacrifice everything to make it all go away – as if it never happened. It's so common to feel, "If I'd only done something differently to prevent this loss, it wouldn't have happened." There was nothing anyone could have done to prevent David's death. So many people asked how I was doing throughout the day of the funeral. I remember saying, "I feel like I'm being carried with great big arms around me; helping me put one foot in front of the other." After the funeral I was soon back home with my family. I realised how incredible the timing of my phone call to him the day of the racing accident, and how incredible the timing of mum and Frank travelling to Toowoomba to see him was. We all have a beautiful memory of our last day of seeing him and talking to him. Good memories are important to hold onto.

The depression stage comes over us when we start facing our present reality of the loss experienced. Understandably, this realisation can lead to intense sadness and despair. This intense sadness I saw firsthand after the loss of David with our mum. Mum was exhausted, vulnerable, she got confused and couldn't get her words out properly. She didn't want to move on, she wasn't hungry and didn't want to eat. She wasn't able or willing to get ready for the day; she wasn't able to enjoy anything. Even though it relates to the grieving process, it was incredibly overwhelming. I watched Mum go through this stage and I felt helpless, as did her husband Frank.

I was sad for a very long time. When the reality of his death hit me, I had many days where I just cried. Some friends didn't know what to do, nor what to say. When I went to church, people didn't come near me. Maybe, I suppose, it was because I was pretending I was OK. This was probably the case because I was good at doing that. But deep down inside I was crumbling under the pain of my loss. I went to a meeting at church and I sat there thinking, "What am I doing here? I shouldn't be here." In hindsight I should've stayed home with my children and be with them, but I had conflicting thoughts. I thought, I might as well go; it could be good for me to be around other people. I sat there feeling miserable. That is probably why people didn't ask me how I was doing. They just left me alone. That isn't how we should respond to someone going through grief. No matter how we may come across, we need to reassure people by saying, "I'm thinking of you in this time," or "I'm praying for you at this time" or just muster up the courage to provide someone with space and time to cry on your shoulder. It's not a weakness to grieve; it's courageous to show you are hurting and struggling.

Church life was busy. Raising two kids at the time and being involved like we were, I didn't grieve my brother's death well. I didn't give myself time to grieve. I was caught up in the busyness of life; trying to help everyone else in my family grieve, while at the same time pastoring the people I served. Even though I was sad, the expression of sadness was put on hold. I didn't allow myself to enjoy my children playing in the backyard, laughing and giggling while making their mud pies. When life and people want to move you on from your sorrow and grief, we must be courageous enough to say, "When I am ready" and give yourself permission to grieve in your time frame, not theirs. Not long after David's funeral, just a couple of weeks later, I turned thirty years old. I still don't remember my thirtieth birthday at all – it's a blur. It was a turning of an age I should've been celebrating, but it was an age I turned that I wanted to forget. I remember a friend threw a small celebration for me and honestly, I don't remember it. I just remember the horrible blue tracksuit I wore while everyone else was dressed up. It was an outward expression showing I wasn't OK.

I had to learn how to cry and tell myself it's OK. Growing up, I was told not to cry, because crying was a weakness. Only those people who were weak cried. I'd feel judged if I cried and vulnerable. But crying allows us to let out an emotion that shouldn't be bottled up on the inside of our souls. It's healthy to cry just as much as it's healthy to laugh: they are emotions that are required to stay healthy emotionally. Tears are medicine for our soul.

The acceptance stage is about how we acknowledge the loss, how we learn to live with the loss and how we readjust our lives to the loss. It was a while after my brother's death that my mind was ready to acknowledge what had happened. But what mattered to me was my family and close friends; friends I could reach out to and seek comfort from. I needed friendships to help me talk about normal things instead of how I was feeling all the time, to help me laugh over the silliest things, to help me play board games with my kids and listen to them argue and fight over who was cheating and who wasn't. It kept my life feeling somewhat normal as I kept walking through the pain.

Sometimes we may also feel like we accept the loss at times, like "Actually, this is alright, I am good and I feel OK" and then before you know it, you revert to another stage of grief again. I was grocery shopping one day a few months after the funeral and I went to get some "red delicious" apples to put in a bag. I picked up one apple and started to cry. I left my trolley with the food in it and went straight home with my children. Our eldest son said to me when we got home, "Mummy, it's OK to cry." He took my hand as I sat on our lounge chair, he cuddled up to me and said, "I cry all the time and you give me lots of hugs and kisses." Well, at that point we all cried and there were lots of cuddles all around.

My faith was challenged through my loss. I doubted God that He was even there with me through it all. But it only made me stronger in my belief in a loving and gracious God as I searched for Him in my grief.

It has been twenty-seven years since my brother died at the age of twenty-seven. Rest in peace my little brother.

My Sister

"We understand death only when it has placed its hands on someone we love" – Madame Germaine deStael

My sister Fiona died suddenly in her sleep.

My sister took a different path in life. She'd often say, "I'm just like my father." She'd say that over and over and she did become just like Dad – an alcoholic and abusive. She was sexually abused when she was just out of nappies. John did things to her that he didn't do to me. His depravity was on another level with my sister and that's not to excuse what he did to me whatsoever. I tried to help my sister as much as I could: she needed professional help to manage the depth of her pain. She developed an addiction to multiple substances, alcohol, drugs and it got worse over time. She would be sober for a little while then start drinking again; creating a vicious cycle in her life. Sometimes, she managed to get cleaned up for a couple of weeks or a couple of months. But then one night she went to a nightclub. She got heavily intoxicated. The person she was with took her home and put her into bed. She died that night in her sleep. I didn't get to say goodbye to my sister. My final words to her a couple of weeks before was during an argument about her destructive life.

She passed away at the age of thirty-eight in the same month thirteen years after David passed away on 31 July 2009.

July always reminds me of their deaths in different ways.

Fiona's death brought so much sadness and anger because her death could have been avoided. She was on a path of complete destruction. I'd often say, "If only she would get help and actually just listen to someone, then she'd still be alive today." Fiona carried so much pain from our childhood. Her pain was written all over her: when she spoke, how she behaved, how she looked. Everything about her was a picture of pain. She thought the only way to get through life and cope with her pain was the same way our dad did.

We eventually got her into a rehab centre in South Australia and she agreed to go. As we were driving her there, she said that she didn't want to go. One of the fundamental rules is that the addict must be willing and want to get help. We tried to reason with her, but she made us turn around and take her back home. We couldn't go through with it because she didn't want to.

She didn't want to take responsibility for her life, so she stayed on the roller coaster of addiction. There are so many stories, so many events that took place, so many times I would just think, "How much more can her body take?"

One thing is for sure: the alcohol and drugs were her enemy. They weren't her friend. Her complete dependence on them changed her physical appearance, her mind, her will, her emotions, her behaviour and in the end, her capacity to survive. Fiona lived every single hour of every day controlled by her childhood trauma.

My sister was bent on doing it her way. People on the outside looking in, blamed me and Mum for not doing enough to help her. But they only saw what was happening from a distant external view; they didn't see what was happening within the family unit. They didn't see her passed out in her lounge room while her small children were running around naked and getting into the kitchen cupboards trying to find something to eat. They didn't see me and Gary breaking into her home to rescue the kids, dress them and bring them back to a safe haven. They didn't hear the fits of rage when she called us, completely inebriated, all hours of the night and day. They didn't hear the death threats we got every day; they didn't witness the hours upon hours we would sit with her and try to empower her to seek help. They didn't witness her clean and sober and then revert backwards falling even deeper each time.

We tried many times over to get her help, to the point where I was confident in the fact that we did every possible thing we could. But you can't help someone who doesn't want to be helped. Fiona didn't want to hear the truth that she needed help. She would revert from victim to thinking she could overcome it all on her own. "Addiction," "dependence," "misuse," "abuse" – whatever you want to call it – it doesn't work like that. It's hundred percent totally and completely all-consuming and the victim must acknowledge that they need help.

When I was seven years old, I'd get her dinner, run a bath for her, comfort her, keep her safe. It was devastating being at her funeral and frustrating that she died like she did.

I went from being angry straight on down to the bargaining stage. I was angry that a life was taken too soon for a reason that could have been helped and then questioning everything I could have done to help prevent her death. I didn't speak at my sister's funeral; I didn't have the emotional capacity at the time to bring her Eulogy. I am forever grateful for the minister who led her funeral that day. He knew her personally. He was honest, wise, gentle and I thank him. You spoke the truth that day – a truth my family needed to hear.

When the truth is exposed, the secret can't have a hold on you anymore. The truth needs to be said for healing to start its journey. Many people the day of the funeral got an understanding of what had been taking place and they said sorry to me and my mum that day for not being more understanding. Those words brought healing.

All I was concerned about were her five children; five of the most resilient, beautiful children who had just lost their mother. I sat down with her children beside me and on my lap: they were all so brave. They were all I could think about that day and I don't remember anything else taking place other than my concern for them.

When we were going through some photos of my sister weeks after her funeral, I remember saying, "She had the most incredible smile." When she smiled, it would light up the whole place. Fiona, in her sober days, would light up any person's life with her smile. I still miss that smile to this day. It's so important that as we grieve the loss of loved ones, that we remember the good times and not always the bad. Whether it's a smile, or the way they laugh – it helps us heal, no matter how sad or ugly their life had been.

I was so angry at myself. I would go over and over in my mind how I could have helped her more. Until one day, I just stopped blaming myself. She had ample opportunity to become well again. How does dragging a victim of addiction by their hair to rehab help? Honestly, I'd love to see the research, because that was the one and only option any one of us had left. And then what? You have a woman in complete anguish, complete pain, complete denial with limited emotional development at thirty eight years of age and a lifetime of trauma to cope with.

Loving someone doesn't always look like the warm fuzzy emotions we give each other. Loving someone sometimes means telling them the truth in love and then letting them go so they can heal.

I then began to be sad. I cried so much. I had lost David and now Fiona. I couldn't believe that I was the only one left. I didn't understand how I could be the only one left. I was grieving on multiple levels. I would think of Mum and my dad; losing two of their children. Their pain, I thought, was so much more than what I was going through. The pain of losing a child before their old age brings so much pain for any parent.

Dad didn't attend Fiona's funeral; he actually didn't believe she died having lived the way she did. He said we were all lying and paid a private investigator to find out what had happened. I kid you not. He lived in constant denial of anything in his life. My aunty (my father's sister) called me and when I'd told her what had happened to my sister, she said she'd let my father know. Mum couldn't talk about Fiona's death for a long time. Over time, it brought up David's death as well. I said to her, "What are the beautiful things about my brother and sister that you remember?" I tried to get her to focus on the good things and not the bad (which is what I did too). For both of us, my sister's death brought back memories of my brother's death. That is a very common occurrence and it is very normal.

Even though I went through some of the stages of grief, unlike my brother's death I gave myself permission and time to grieve her death. Even though there were pressures, such as work and family, I was determined to grieve well this time (or at least, as well as I could). I didn't attend everything on my schedule, I allowed myself time. I kept a journal, I kept company, I focused on my children and my husband.

Like many people who face loss, we got through the loss of my sister with the love and support of each other, putting our grievances behind us. Death can bring so many uncertainties and we never know how we will actually feel when we face loss. Until we're faced with it, we can't really know for certain how those feelings will affect us. Death can bring people together or it can drive people apart – we have the responsibility to allow either one to take place.

I don't believe time heals everything, because time can fester things and make things worse too; making us more angry or sad. But I do believe that over time we can heal if we allow ourselves the time to heal.

I learned to give myself permission to grieve and to heal over time.

My Father

There came a time for me to distance myself and my children from my dad. When my daughter was eleven years old, my father called, drunk as usual and started yelling at her on the phone, calling her all the names under the sun. She gave me the phone and said, "I think Grandad's drunk again. He is swearing and is very angry at me. I don't know what I've done to make him so angry." I took the phone and said, "That was Steffany you were speaking to, not me." He used to call all hours of the night and early morning. Every time the phone would go at ridiculous times throughout the night, one of us would get out of bed and answer it. As ministers in a church, we never knew who it could be that needed our help. Gary answered the phone this one early morning: it was 2am.

Dad was out of control. Gary told him he needed help with his alcohol problem and Dad responded, "I don't have a problem with alcohol." To Dad, it was everyone else's problem even though he was the one abusive on the phone at 2am. That morning we made the decision that we didn't want him in our children's lives any longer. That was the day I drew a line in the sand and said, "No More Dad."

Since that day we kept our children from seeing their grandad and our children have thanked us for that decision. Our oldest son said, "As grandchildren, we didn't experience a lot of his abusive ways." We stopped the pain and the abuse from my father repeating the cycle in our children's childhood. There's a time for everything to take place. Even though our children didn't see him or hear from him, I made sure I kept in contact with him. I always knew what he was up to and where he was.

My father passed away in 2021 and in 2020 just before the world stopped with Covid 19, I called him, to tell him I loved him. That is when he told me he had Cirrhosis of the liver and colon cancer and a lot of other ailments in his body which I was already aware of. We had many conversations by phone until his death in April 2021. He didn't want me to be involved at his funeral because he knew I would mention things about his life he never wanted mentioning. But it was my aunty, his sister, that asked me to give the eulogy. So, I stood up on the church's platform and began to share from my heart about my father's life. I spoke about how he loved his bird aviaries and his beautiful dogs and then I spoke about his drinking and how he was a very unhappy man.

One of my father's friends at his funeral came up to me after and asked me about Dad. He said, "Did you say that he was an alcoholic?" I said, "He was – all of my life." His friend said that that made perfect sense as to why he was the way he was. He was irrational when he spoke and he had slurred speech and couldn't walk properly – the nerve endings in his feet had gone. This man had thought like so many other people thought: he had had a stroke. But his friend said, "So he didn't have a stroke; he was an alcoholic?" His friend disclosed that he himself was a recovering alcoholic and he always had his suspicions about my father being one.

I was angry about Dad's death. It was OK to be angry; he was a neglectful father, he was a drunk, he was verbally abusive and emotionally demeaning. There was nothing I could do that was ever good enough. I thought I shouldn't be this angry. I wondered why I didn't feel relieved that he was gone. I was a grown woman with adult children and very happy and content. So why did I suddenly feel angry again? I became very quiet trying to gather my thoughts and keep them in perspective. I was navigating again my grieving process.

I decided I needed to talk it through with a professional because despite so many years of healing and overcoming so much horror, I needed to talk about what I was feeling towards my father at this stage of my life. I had seen a counsellor in the past, but my doctor gave me a referral to see a clinical psychologist and said to me, "This lady is qualified in the area of complex trauma and, Nicola, you've experienced trauma on multiple levels throughout your young life. It doesn't hurt to talk it through with a professional." She also added, "I know you've seen someone in the past, but it won't hurt to talk through your anger about your dad."

As I was in the waiting room ready to see the psychologist, I was listening to the calming music being played in the background. It wasn't anything mystical or magical, it was just so beautifully calming. She came out and invited me into her room, and welcomed me, "Hello Nicola. You may sit wherever you like." I entered and sat down on her lounge. She sat on the opposite lounge, then proceeded to ask me how I was and at that very moment, I just cried and I cried, and I cried. Yet, it didn't faze her at all. She didn't jump up to console me, she didn't display fear. She was so calm and patient. I kept apologising for crying, but she said, "Don't apologise, just let it all out."

I don't recall ever allowing myself to just cry like that. I didn't realise I had so much just locked up inside of me. I want to emphasise that I was in a safe place; no one judging or criticising me, no one telling me to calm down, no one telling me to get a grip, no one looking at me as if I was peculiar and no one talking about me behind my back (which I had experienced a lot of). She wasn't associated with anyone I knew, and nothing was going to get back to the people I knew. This was for me: this was my time to sit, relax and talk and get some new understanding about my anger. In the past, I would have a little cry, then suck it up and move on with my life. To everyone on the outside, I was OK. That happened all throughout my life. Mum didn't like us crying. She'd tell us to stop it or she'd give us something to really cry about. I needed to just let it all out and with that came immense relief. It was like a huge mountain being lifted off me for the very first time. I didn't realise how heavy that mountain was.

Dad could have been such a great man to his family and friends. I was grieving for something I never had: a loving father. I had to see him for who he really was – a broken human being. Even though I knew that in my heart, I recognised it as I spoke about his death out loud. I didn't want to hate Dad and carry bitterness. I wanted to love him and even though throughout the years I told him I loved him, I was struggling to feel that love now. Going through this stage of anger helped me get perspective of who he was. I was able to finally put him to rest in my heart and when I did that, I was at peace with myself.

The Bible says, "Blessed are those that mourn, for they shall be comforted." – Matthew 5:4

The Dash Poem by Linda Ellis

I read of a man who stood to speak,

At the funeral of a friend,

He referred to the dates on the tombstone,

From beginning to the end.

He noted that first came the date of birth,

And spoke the following date with tears,

But he said what mattered most of all,

Was the dash between those years.

For that dash represents all the time,

That they spent alive on earth,

And now only those who loved them,

know what that little line is worth.

For it matters not, how much we won,

The cars, the house, the cash,

What matters is how we live and love,

And how we spend our dash.

So, think about this long and hard:

Are there things you'd like to change?

For you never know much time is left,

That can still be rearranged.

If we could just slow down enough,

To consider what's true and real,

And always try to understand,

The way other people feel.

And be less quick to anger,

And show appreciation more,

And love the people in our lives,

Like we've never loved before.

If we treat each other with respect,

And more often wear a smile,

Remembering this special dash,

Might only last a little while.

So, when your eulogy is being read,

With your life's actions to rehash,

Would you be; proud of the things they say,

About how you spent YOUR dash?"

INVISIBLE SCARS

NICOLA RUCCI

PART TWO

I've learned that trauma changes the brain; but so does healing.

Chapter 5
WHAT DOES RESEARCH SAY

Our lives can't be condensed into a handful of pages. Each trauma, tragedy or triumph we experience is loaded with emotions, thoughts and consequences that we could never record in a short book. But my hope is that I've shared enough of my story, in order for you – or someone close to you – to be able to identify with my journey.

I want to be intentionally helpful in this next part: The following chapters outline some truths and principles that were instrumental to my personal restoration. They've helped me and include an opportunity for you to reflect on these principles for your own life. I sincerely hope you find them helpful too. I encourage you to purchase a journal so that you can record your thoughts, prayers and reflections. Personally, I've found this to be an invaluable tool over the last thirty-five years of my life. There's something powerful about writing out your emotions and thoughts and bringing them into the light.

As a church minister and Christ follower, I've learnt I can't help people with their trauma if first I haven't been helped myself: It's hard to help people from a place of brokenness. I certainly don't have all the answers and I'm not a qualified psychologist. I recognise my limitations to listen, pray for the person and then guide them to a professional in the field. I think it's important to keep a list of people, doctors, clinical psychologists, psychiatrists, social workers and counsellors that can help the healing process for people who come to us for help.

Even in my own experiences and in my own healing journey I still can't take someone the entire way – and that's OK. Our role isn't to control the healing outcome for those people. Seeing a psychologist opened the heart of my understanding that my "complex trauma" needed more than a church minister. In saying that, I think it's crucial we do our research: We need to be able to put words to what we've experienced, know the symptoms, the triggers and the prevalence. Why? Because it's empowering and knowledge is empowering – not just for us but also for others.

So, what does research say?

Firstly, I'd like to say that I know we don't want to know the statistics concerning childhood sexual abuse. We don't want to know how many children are being abused each day. We want to envision children in a safe and secure environment. We don't naturally gravitate to information that depicts a child's life in these horrific circumstances. I'm not arguing that it should be normalised either: We should never get to the point where we are desensitised as a society to hearing of the mistreatment and abuse of children. But I do think it's important to know about what's happening in our communities (wherever that is for you). We can make a difference and change can only occur when information is exposed and when the masses work together to protect children from harm. Our children should be of utmost priority in all areas of their young lives.

Alcohol Use

Around eighty percent of Australian adults have consumed alcohol at some time.[1] Drinking alcohol isn't a taboo: It's understood as an accepted behaviour in our Australian society and is even a large part of our Australian culture; the after-work glass of wine, the afternoon beers, the pool side bubbly. Being intoxicated isn't looked down upon either, because it's a cultural norm; an entitlement for hard work and a means for celebration (like coming of age). The Global Drug Survey[2] revealed that drinking to feel drunk was highest in Australia when compared to the reported global average. So, it isn't wrong to say that on a global scale, Australia exhibits the highest population of heavy drinkers. The Alcohol and Drug Foundation goes on to say that it can often be seen as *"unAustralian"* to abstain from alcohol. Yet concerningly, nation-wide, alcohol addiction (also known as "substance use disorder"), is a personal struggle for one in twenty individuals.[3] The National Alcohol Strategy writes that one in four Australians "are drinking alcohol at risky levels." Alcohol also underpins

---

[1] Alcohol and Drug Foundation. 2020, p.5. *National Alcohol Strategy.* https://www.health.gov.au/sites/default/files/documents/2020/11/national-alcohol-strategy-2019-2028.pdf

[2] The Global Drug Survey. 2021, p. 17. *GDS 2021 Global Report.* https://www.globaldrugsurvey.com/wp-content/uploads/2021/12/Report2021_global.pdf

[3] Healthdirect Australia. 2023, p.1. *Substance Abuse.* https://www.healthdirect.gov.au/substance-abuse#:~:text=Around%201%20in%2020%20Australians,counselling%20throug h%20to%20hospital%20treatment

four thousand drug-related deaths a year and is associated with twenty-nine percent of family violence cases, as it is with intimate partner violence at thirty-five percent.

In the US, it was revealed by the Substance Abuse and Mental Health Services Administration (SAMHSA)[4] that about "6.1 million children under the age of seventeen" lived in a home where one parent had an alcohol addiction. In addition, about "1.4 million children" lived with a single parent who also struggles with alcohol. The National Centre of Substance Abuse and Child Welfare[5] maintained that around 38.9 percent of child removal cases, where the children were removed from their parent's care, was due to the parents' alcohol or drug abuse.

As I've shared in my story, there's a lot more to the issue of parents abusing alcohol than what you might see at first glance. When a parent is struggling with addiction, it's connected to complicated dynamics and challenges that can span generations. It takes a lot of effort and commitment to change these patterns and start a new, healthier way of life. Nevertheless, a family challenged by substance abuse is characterised by "an environment of secrecy, loss, conflict, violence or abuse, emotional

---

[4] Lipari & Van Horn. 2017, p.3. *Children Living with Parents who have a Substance Use Disorder.* https://www.samhsa.gov/data/sites/default/files/report_3223/ShortReport-3223.html

[5] The National Centre of Substance Abuse and Child Welfare. 2019, p.1. *Child Welfare and Alcohol and Drug Use* Statistics. https://ncsacw.acf.hhs.gov/research/child-welfare-and-treatment-statistics.aspx#:~:text=When%20calculating%20the%20national%20average,an%20identified%20condition%20for%20removal

chaos, role reversal, and fear."[6] Parental substance abuse significantly impacts the child and poses a much higher risk of harm occurring. As parents we have the role of providing a consistent, stable, predictable and safe environment for our children, enabling us to be responsive both physically and emotionally. However, our capacity to do so is significantly reduced when there's substance abuse – especially when complicated issues of domestic violence, divorce, housing, unemployment or mental health problems are thrown into the mix.[7][8][9][10][11]

---

[6] Lander, Howsare & Byrne. 2013. *The Impact of Substance Use Disorders on Families and Children: From Theory to Practice.* https://www.ncbi.nlm.nih.gov/pmc/articles/PMC3725219/

[7] Australian Institute of Health and Wellness. 2008, p.1. *Improving Outcomes for Children Living in Families with Parental Substance Misuse: What do we know and what should we do?* https://aifs.gov.au/resources/policy-and-practice-papers/improving-outcomes-children-living-families-parental-substance

[8] Australian Institute of Health and Wellness. 2022, p.1. *National Framework for Protecting Australia's Children Indicators.* https://www.aihw.gov.au/reports/child-protection/nfpac/contents/national-framework-indicators/3-2-parental-substance-use-alcohol

[9] Goldberg & Blaauw. 2019, p.1. *Parental Substance Use Disorder and Child Abuse: Risk Factors for Child Maltreatment?* https://www.tandfonline.com/doi/full/10.1080/13218719.2019.1664277

[10] Administration for Children & Families. 2019. *Is There a Link between Parental Drug Use and the Prevalence of Child Maltreatment and/or the Increase in the Number of Children in Foster Care?* https://www.acf.hhs.gov/cb/faq/can13

[11] American Academy of Experts in Traumatic Stress. 2020, p.2. *Effects of Parental Substance Abuse on Children and Families.* https://www.aaets.org/traumatic-stress-library/effects-of-parental-substance-abuse-on-children-and-families

Everything we do as parents has a flow on effect. Unfortunately,[12] "children of substance abusing parents show increased risk for emotional, behavioural, and social problems." Although not every child will experience consequences or come into harm, parental substance abuse places the child in an environment that poses increased risks (Lipari & Van Horn). There isn't only a higher likelihood of experiencing emotional, physical and sexual abuse, children living in these circumstances may experience more physical, mental and emotional health problems than other children. They may experience unstable living situations, poverty or health issues (Administration for Children & Families).

According to the American Academy of Experts in Traumatic Stress, such family circumstances create an environment of unpredictable behaviour accompanied by vague communication. This can lead to the child experiencing a lack of structure and non-existent rules and boundaries, confusion and insecurity, concern, anger and blame. Only a few children come to realise that they can't control their parents. It can impact a child's social life, their development, academic attendance and performance, and their mental health. All of this impacts the child's potential to experience and develop trusting and secure relationships as they grow older. A negative consequence of parental substance abuse is the child growing to be too emotionally responsible for others and adapting to adult roles, far younger than appropriate for their age (also known as "parentification") (Lander, Howsare & Byrne). This accurately depicts my experience growing up as I "parented" my parents for a very long

---

[12] Solis, Shadur, Burns & Hussong. 2012. *Understanding the Diverse Needs of Children whose Parents Abuse Substances.* https://www.ncbi.nlm.nih.gov/pmc/articles/PMC3676900/

time and parented my brother and sister when I was only a child myself.

Child abuse and neglect

To define child abuse and neglect, I turn to the term "child maltreatment." The World Health Organisation[13] understands child maltreatment as exhibiting four different types of abuse: physical abuse, sexual abuse, emotional and psychological abuse and defines child maltreatment as the following:

"All forms of physical and/or emotional ill-treatment, sexual abuse, neglect or negligent treatment or commercial or other exploitation, resulting in actual or potential harm to the child's health, survival, development or dignity in the context of a relationship of responsibility, trust or power."

Thousands of incidents of child abuse are unreported, but "every 11 minutes" in Australia, a child suffers neglect or abuse of sexual, emotional or physical nature. It almost always occurs by someone they know and likely trust, and almost always in their place of residence.[14]

---

[13] World Health Organisation. 2006, p.10. *Preventing Child Maltreatment: A Guide to Taking Action and Generating Evidence*. https://www.who.int/publications/i/item/preventing-child-maltreatment-a-guide-to-taking-action-and-generating-evidence

[14] Act for Kids. *Child Abuse and Neglect in Australia*. https://www.actforkids.com.au/the-issue/#:~:text=There%20were%2049%2C690%20confirmed%20cases%20of%20child%20abuse,to%20trust%3B%20most%20often%20in%20their%20own%20home

Child Sexual Abuse

I likewise turn to the WHO's definition of sexual abuse:

"Sexual abuse is defined as the involvement of a child in sexual activity that he or she does not fully comprehend, is unable to give informed consent to, or for which the child is not developmentally prepared, or else that violates the laws or social taboos of society. Children can be sexually abused by both adults and other children who are – by virtue of their age or stage of development – in a position of responsibility, trust, or power over the victim."

According to Blue Knot Foundation, in Australia "one in three girls and one in six boys are sexually abused before the age of eighteen.[15] Further, reported by the Australian Bureau of Statistics, the average age of childhood sexual abuse occurring is as young as "8.8 years." Unfortunately, adults who were abused as children are twice as likely to face violence and three times more likely to experience violence from a partner, compared to those who weren't abused as children.[16]

"Sexual violence breaks every social convention relating to sexuality." - Evelyne Josse

The impact of sexual abuse isn't only psychological or physical, but it also affects the individual's whole life, their

---

[15] Blue Knot. 2021. *Facts and Figures.* https://blueknot.org.au/resources/facts-and-figures/

[16] Australian Bureau of Statistics. 2019. *Characteristics and Outcomes of Child Abuse.* https://www.abs.gov.au/articles/characteristics-and-outcomes-childhood-abuse

perceived sense of self, their physical and social life, their relationships and right down to their financial circumstances.[17] I truly believe that such a violation impacts how we perceive ourselves and how we perceive others to perceive us. Sexual abuse attacks our sense of dignity, our sense of honour; it destroys our self-confidence and self-esteem. Even though I've always had a fight in my spirit, I used to lack self confidence in so many ways. The violation that I experienced as a child made me feel ugly on the inside: I'd look in the mirror and tell myself "You're ugly."

Emotional and Psychological Abuse

WHO defines emotional and psychological abuse as the following:

"Emotional and psychological abuse involves both isolated incidents, as well as a pattern of failure over time on the part of a parent or caregiver to provide a developmentally appropriate and supportive environment. Acts in this category may have a high probability of damaging the child's physical or mental health, or its physical, mental, spiritual, moral or social development. Abuse of this type includes: the restriction of movement; patterns of belittling, blaming, threatening, frightening, discriminating against or ridiculing; and other non-physical forms of rejection or hostile treatment."

---

[17] Australian Institute of Family Studies. 2011, p.1. *The Impacts of Sexual Assault on Women.* https://aifs.gov.au/resources/practice-guides/impacts-sexual-assault-women

Trauma

"Trauma isn't the story of something that happened back then, [trauma is] the current imprint of that pain, horror, and fear living inside..." - Bessel Van Der Kolk

I was recently gifted a book by my daughter called, "The Body Keeps the Score" by Bessel Van Der Kolk. The book accurately provides an in depth understanding of trauma and how trauma impacts our entire being, our mind, brain, and our body and how it's all connected. It explains that trauma is an event that's so intense, it changes how our brain processes and remembers past experiences. When a child or young person goes through multiple traumatic events repeatedly, often caused by their parent or caregiver, it can impact different parts of the child's development and have a large impact on their self-image. In turn, it directly affects their ability to build safe, secure relationships with others and can harm their physical and mental health. When the child grows up, the buildup of this trauma over their lives leads to many complicated issues related to the trauma and is referred to as complex trauma.[18]

I want to explain trauma responses because for me, trauma responses are a huge part of my lived experience: Firstly, it's normal to have intense physical, mental, emotional or behavioural responses after a distressing event. Over a few weeks your mind and body should settle and your responses will lessen. It's important to consider speaking with a professional, like a counsellor GP or psychologist if you find that after a month you're

---

[18] The National Child Traumatic Stress Network. *Complex Trauma.* https://www.nctsn.org/what-is-child-trauma/trauma-types/complex-trauma

not feeling like you used to prior to the event.[19] However, sometimes a traumatic event can have a long-term impact on our psychological, physical, social and spiritual self. A trauma response is our reaction to the intense event that has taken place. Our response may be an emotional reaction, physical reaction or mental or behavioural. Our responses may be feelings of overwhelm, panic attacks, flashbacks, feelings of un-safety or needing to leave the situation immediately.[20]

These responses are unique to every individual, as are the triggers that invoke our response. These triggers are understood by our brains as threatening which causes our trauma responses. Triggers manifest in numerous ways, but they could take form as a particular smell like a perfume, a song on the radio, certain times of the year or specific dates, places like a bathroom or a bedroom, a person that reminds you of someone from your past, an argument that gives you the same physical feeling from your past or maybe simply being in a crowded place (Psych Central). Personally, I was triggered by certain smells and different times of the year, especially when the seasons started to change. I also hated getting into lifts at the shopping mall because small spaces made me feel insecure as a child: I was abused in small spaces.

"Our body holds onto trauma; it responds to traumas experiences and will make us sick." - Bessel Van Der Kolk

---

[19] Better Health Channel. 2021, p.1. *Trauma: Reaction and Recovery.* https://www.betterhealth.vic.gov.au/health/conditionsandtreatments/trauma-reaction-and-recovery

[20] Psych Central. 2022. *What is Trauma?* https://psychcentral.com/health/what-is-trauma

Importantly, The Body Keeps the Score, provided me with the understanding of how my physical self, my body, has also held onto my traumatic experiences and the manifestation of this consequence is illness. I was diagnosed with Hashimoto's Thyroid disease later in life and even though it can be hereditary, my doctor explained that it can lay dormant for many years waiting for the right time to surface. Just as you experience increased stress or shock, it can emerge.

For years I heard sermons about the disciples falling asleep in the Garden of Gethsemane because they were lazy or slack. They couldn't pray for an hour because they were tired and failed to understand the importance of the moment, they were living in. But the Gospel reveals a different story. He records the same instance with a very interesting truth. In Luke 22:45 he says they were "sleeping from sorrow." The Bible says we are tripartite beings: We are one person made up of three parts – body, soul and spirit which can't be separated (1 Thessalonians 5:23). Each component affects the other. When we're happy, we laugh. When we celebrate, we jump and shout giving everyone high fives. When we're oppressed, we're sick. When we're worried, we can't sleep. When we're angry, we could become violent.

I've learned that trauma changes the brain; but so does healing. Healing looks different for everyone: there's no "one size fits all." We've all been created differently and uniquely.

Trauma doesn't just heal by itself: You have to be intentional and work through the process. Otherwise, trauma will come back and cause more damage than the event itself.

Personal Reflection

1. Are you carrying trauma in your body? Please describe it.

2. When was the last time you spoke to a doctor about your physical ailments? Why?

3. What issues have created a tapestry of trauma in your life? Can you list them?

4. Which issues are currently causing you to respond or react in ways that you regret? Can you list them?

5. In what ways has this chapter helped you?

Personal Promise

I will get through the trauma in my life one step at a time.

Come out from under the label of victim and walk towards being victorious.

Chapter 6
OUR VULNERABILITY OPENS THE DOOR TO HEALING

"To share your weakness is to make yourself vulnerable. To make yourself vulnerable, is to show your strength."

– Criss Jami

Vulnerability is being courageous, even when you don't want to be.

An egg can't be used until it's cracked open and the shell removed: only then can you use it to create delicious food, like cakes, a beautiful loaf of bread or some baked biscuits. In similar ways, unless we have the courage to be vulnerable, all that needs to heal on the inside of us remains buried. It takes courage to be vulnerable in this world; this world that constantly tells us we aren't good enough. This world hides its imperfections and gives the social media platform an image of perfection. Why is it that we prefer to put on a brave face, just to demonstrate to the world around us, that we have it all together? We often don't have it all together, so why do we front as though we do? Because vulnerability is seen as weakness in society. People view it as exposing your dirty laundry out in the open for others to see. People don't like to hear your genuine honesty and openness because if they were to respond truly empathetically it could expose their own inner darkness that they try so hard to cover up. When I began to open up and share my story about my childhood, I was told to be quiet. I was told that people don't want to hear those things and they won't want to be around me anymore and will think that I'm a disgusting person. My mother grew up like that too: she was always taught the rhetoric "children should be seen and not heard." She had to be quiet and not speak out of turn or speak up for herself.

It was normal to grow up in a family that kept secrets. My grandfather never spoke about the atrocities that he experienced happening in the war. He used to say, "We don't talk of such things in this home." Veterans experience deep pain from the atrocities of war and the horrors of loss. When I've spoken with other people (veterans, or family and friends of veterans), they say it's not spoken of because they couldn't imagine anyone understanding, relating or even responding in a way that validates their experience. It also brings back the excruciating pain they'd experienced.

But when we don't share our thoughts and feelings, we can't begin to deal with the hidden trauma inside of us. Some psychologists say that we numb vulnerability by keeping everything hidden, by keeping all our hardships buried deep within us or sent to a box in our mind. In doing this, we unconsciously experience a loss of the power of vulnerability, a loss of how that could bring healing to our lives.

The opposite of our fear is love; the opposite of pain and heartache is joy. By not sharing and allowing ourselves to open up to others and vice versa, we in actual fact stop living the joy-filled life we were meant to live. Vulnerability teaches us to love, it teaches us compassion and it keeps our hearts soft towards people. When someone is vulnerable with me and shares what they're going through and how they're feeling, it automatically helps me understand why they are the way they are. If it's pertinent to the conversation, I can often say, "I relate to your pain and hurt." I can also help them on their healing journey by saying, "This is how I began to deal with the pain and the hurt in my life. Maybe it can help you."

It is utterly terrifying to think about being open and transparent about past hurts: especially abuse of any kind. We run the risk of being hurt again. This is why for so many people, they never deal with the pain of their past trauma. It's important not to rush someone to open up, but to be patient with them and allow them to take their time when they're ready. This is of utmost priority to the person. They must be and feel valued.

If we're going to start our healing journey, then we'll need to be open and transparent one slow step at a time. I know it's a scary thought but stay with me. When I talk about my vulnerability, I'm talking about exposing the secrets and the dark areas that happened to me in my life; exposing the times of my life that were meant to be pure and innocent but were turned into horror. Even if you didn't experience what I went through, the transparency of our heart on many levels has the power to release others to open up and share their stories. But I also feel compelled to say, when you begin to share your story, some will hate you for it, some will mock you, judge you, and see you as a liability. Some will see you sharing and being your true authentic self as a weakness; others will react to you simply for being honest. Your vulnerability will expose insecurities and they may just throw everything back in your face treating you like a victim. Some friendships will end; some family members won't believe you. But, by the same token, some will draw closer to you, friendships will flourish, family will fight for you, and people will remove a mask that is hiding their own shame, guilt, and condemnation. They will feel free to go on their own healing journey.

"Being our messy, imperfect, authentic selves help create a space where others feel safe to be themselves too. Your vulnerability can be a gift to others. How badass is that!" – Brittin Oakman

It's very wise to find a trusted person or persons that will hold your heart delicately and highly valued. Our vulnerability belongs in an intimate space that is safe. This safe space can be created by two or three people, two or three friends or two or three family members. Our vulnerability actually means being open to injury. That is why it's so important to seek out trusted people.

We don't live in a perfect world. I'm not perfect, you aren't perfect and the people in your life aren't perfect. It's easy to see others as having the perfect life when we're living in such a horrible mess. It's human to think we're the only ones in the world that must be going through what we're going through. When you begin to open up about the issues weighing deep in your soul, then your heart wakes up to the fact that you aren't alone and you begin to build friendships on a much deeper level. That's the power of vulnerability.

"Listening is much more than allowing another to talk while waiting for a chance to respond. Listening is paying full attention to others and welcoming them into our very beings." – Henri Nouwen

We all need somebody who listens to us and we need to learn how to listen as well. One of the most powerful tools we can give someone is a listening ear. Why? Because our hearing as well as our touch are the last senses to leave us when we die. Listening is a fine art these days, but when you have someone in your life that listens more than they speak, then they have the capacity to truly hear, truly learn and understand your circumstances and who you are before they advise. Providing a listening ear isn't just hearing. Hearing is passive; listening is active. It's often said that when someone listens, it's an act of love.

For example: when you ask your kids to come to the dinner table because dinner is ready, you hear utter silence. Then you tell them again, maybe a little louder, giving them the benefit of not hearing the first time. This time you hear a grunt. Then you yell and tell them to get their backsides to the dinner table or they'll miss out on dinner. Familiar? They then come running to the table, don't they? They were hearing with passivity until they listened and acted upon it. And don't worry! They always came running to eat their dinner. They never missed out on their dinner. They were always too hungry!

People need people. We can't grow in isolation, living a life without any people in it because of deep hurt. Healing can't take place with just you and your trauma talking to you about your trauma. Isolation will only reinforce our pain and will keep our soul in hurt.

We need others who have been there, who understand why we say the things we do and how we can overcome. Getting advice from those who are a step ahead of us is one of the greatest strategies in our healing journey. In this case, we don't need to be afraid to share our weaknesses or our perceived failures, because this person has travelled the same roads (or similar ones); dealing with their greatest fears and strengthening those weak areas that tried to stop them from moving forward.

Some people will come into your life at different stages of your healing journey. Someone will be there in the initial stage of you opening up about what took place. Then someone else will come into your life and take you a little further. Then someone else will come for a season. I don't believe there's one and only one person for the whole journey. It's healthy to have different people along the way.

Proverbs 11:14 says, "Where there is no counsel, the people fall; but in the multitude of counsellors there is safety."

Less is more when we entrust our heart to someone. I made many mistakes in this area of my life because I didn't want to hold onto the pain any longer. So I told someone who was a friend and they told me to just get over it. I felt embarrassed, humiliated and that ugly feeling of shame reared its head again. I felt exposed, I shared information with her about my abuse and she didn't hold my heart in a safe space. I learnt that lesson as I got older and began to wise up with the people around me. I eventually found a couple of incredible women whom I could trust with my story.

One of those ladies became a good friend and I gave her permission to speak the truth in love to me. She helped me understand why I did the things I did and said the things I said. I become accountable to her for my healing and growth as a woman, a wife, a mother and a friend. She became a mentor and confidant. But to be accountable I had to be teachable; taking responsibility for my future self. You won't grow through your trauma or your life's hardships and you won't heal to the degree you need to heal unless you're willing to hear some hard truths. Those hard truths can hurt you and they can offend you; the hard truths speak directly into your victim mentality. Those hard truths are also freeing. We may not feel that at the time because we see it as being hurt again. However, if we allow ourselves time to heal and trust those who hold our best interests at heart, then we're safe to keep on our journey to healing.

A victim mentality is convinced that everyone is out to deliberately hurt them. They hold onto grudges, resentments, and offences and speak those negative words over their life and onto others. They blame everyone else for their circumstances; not seeing that they can change their situation.

You can't be both Victim and Victor at the same time. Living in victimhood keeps you in your pain. Living in victory says you've overcome the pain.

You can choose to be a victim in your story or you can choose to be the victor. Victimhood stops us moving forward. It focuses its attention on self ("me," "my," and "it's all about me and my pain"). It's a form of self-pity. When we come to see we are completely broken and need help to get through, we can then begin to come out from under the label of victim and walk towards being victorious. One of the key ingredients for me breaking free from my victimhood was forgiveness. Forgiving others and forgiving myself was one of the first steps to becoming a victor in my story. Being open to advice and great counsel from friends, loved ones and a professional counsellor also helped me overcome the victimhood.

Allow God to hold your vulnerability. Your vulnerability is a God-given strength. It's not a weakness to share your heart with someone. Ultimately, we can trust God with our heart: He holds our heart in His intimate space and because of that, He will lead us to a trusted few, who will hold our heart in the same safe intimate space. God will give you the courage and strength to share your pain to those trusted few He's led you to. Trust God with your heart and He won't let you down. Be honest with the real you because there's only one authentic you. Allow for the beautiful you to rise and flourish and never be ashamed of who you are. Be yourself and learn to like you.

"Vulnerability is the birthplace of love, belonging, joy, courage, empathy and creativity. It's the source of hope, empathy, accountability and authenticity." – Brené Brown

Personal Reflection

1. Go ahead: fear nothing, be vulnerable and air your dirty laundry. It's just between you, your journal and God. What would you write?

2. Name those people in your life who are one step ahead of you. They have overcome and are further on their journey towards wholeness than you.

3. Is there one person you trust? Is there one person you feel comfortable to begin talking to?

4. Have you ever considered receiving professional help? Why?

5. In which way has this chapter helped you?

Personal promise

God cares for me. I am courageous. I am victorious.

I will both lie down in peace and sleep; for You alone, O Lord, make me dwell in safety (Psalm 4:8).

Don't let your bitterness become a life sentence.

Chapter 7
THERE'S A TIME FOR FORGIVENESS

"Forgiveness doesn't validate the one who hurt us and it doesn't justify their hurtful actions. Forgiveness saves us. It sets us free!"

As I've spoken about being vulnerable and sharing your heart with a trusted few people (being accountable and then taking responsibility), the next big challenge in my life was to forgive.

I am definitely not the perfect example of someone who can forgive quickly. Forgiveness didn't happen quickly for me and it doesn't have to. Anyone who has suffered abuse like I did, understands forgiveness isn't a quick process.

As I was sitting in a church service with Gary and our friend, the church sermon that day was on forgiveness. I remember just sitting there listening to the words, "God is a loving and just God and He wants us all to forgive and lead a life of freedom through forgiveness." There was great teaching through the word of God that day, but I sat there thinking of all the people I had to forgive and I didn't know where to begin. I knew I had bitterness towards them, because it came out when I spoke and my thoughts were consumed with what happened to me. I was very quick to scathe any man who did harm to any woman. I'd tell people what should happen to such men in society. Those words came out because of the deep pain of my abuse.

How could I rectify all that had happened to me and my siblings, by just forgiving? That was an impossible question going through my mind and one I soon learned was true: I couldn't rectify any of it. Forgiveness wasn't going to erase the damage done to us, but it was going to free me from the hatred which I held onto.

"To forgive is not to excuse what the other person did. It's to prevent their behaviour from destroying your heart." – Trisha Davis

I heard a sermon at church on forgiveness when I was eighteen. I got anxious, because I knew deep down in my heart that I had to forgive but I didn't know how. My heart raced and I wanted to throw up. I was so overwhelmed by the thought, "I have to forgive," that I left the church service not forgiving any of them. I was angry at the minister too, for telling me I had to forgive. He didn't know what I had gone through. He would never understand any of it. These were all things I said afterwards.

Have you heard the old saying, "Forgive and you will forget"? There's some truth in that statement, but not all of us can forget. How could I ever forget the things that happened to me as a child? How was I ever going to block out the images I'd see when they'd come back so viciously in my mind? Especially in times when my defences were down, in times of my frustration and anger, when I was feeling like a failure, my negative thoughts would again speak to me loudly in my ears and my soul. My eighteen-year-old self was trying to figure it all out on her own. I didn't tell Gary everything. He had his own unforgiveness to work through and I also didn't want to burden him with it all. It was something he couldn't help me with anyway, other than give me his listening ear and cry with me.

As the weeks and months went on, in the back of my mind, were the words "forgive." Every time I thought those words, it felt like hard work to do. It didn't feel like it was a comforting and a releasing freeing thing to do – it felt like a chore.

I was angry at the injustice that had been done to me. Anger acknowledges what the abuser has done to you. When it's acknowledged, we then have the opportunity to take responsibility to step forward in our healing journey. Psychological research says that anger needs to take place for healing to take its course. It's one of the stages of grief that needs to be worked through. Our anger is validated, but to stay angry isn't good for our mental health, our emotional wellbeing and our physical body.

Through my journey of forgiveness, I leaned on multiple scriptures. But in order to lean on them, I had to understand them.

"It would be better to be thrown into the sea with a millstone hung around your neck than to cause one of these little ones to fall into sin. So, watch yourselves." – Luke 17:2-3

Jesus warned the oppressors, perpetrators and abusers that they will be answerable and they will be judged by God. In modern days, it means they must come before the court of law and be judged by our judicial system and then ultimately, they will stand before God to be judged when they die.

God hates injustice. If God loves us so much, then I know God hated the violation that took place with me, my sister and the pain inflicted upon my brother and mother.

It's often said time is the healer, but time doesn't always heal our pain and hurt. It can often fester more anger, more anxiety, more frustration and more animosity. That's why there's so much narrative around "forgive quickly or you may become bitter, and bitterness hardens the heart." I needed to know why I was forgiving the person and what I had done to ask for forgiveness. When I've been told by people that I had hurt them, I sometimes found it quick to ask for forgiveness, but when I had to forgive, that was a different story. By doing that, I was being hypocritical in my understanding of the power forgiveness holds.

Matthew 6:14-15 says, "For if you forgive other people when they sin against you, your heavenly Father will also forgive you. But if you do not forgive others their sins, your heavenly Father will not forgive you." I needed this to become a big part in my faith in God. Forgiveness works both ways and sometimes it will feel like you're letting the other person off the hook with what they've done to you.

Jesus gives us the perfect example of what forgiveness is. When He was dying on the cross, He exclaimed, "Father, forgive them, for they don't know what they're doing." – Luke 23:34

Jesus was praying for His enemies; the people that put Him on the cross. What grace and mercy He extended towards all those people! I wanted to live in that grace too. But it was going to require some hard work on my part to get there.

Forgiving someone doesn't mean it now establishes a relationship with that person. It means they don't hold the power of revenge, hatred and bitterness that's going on in your heart anymore. When we forgive, we take back the control from those who hold it. Forgiveness doesn't change the past, but it can enlarge your future.

If the person repents even to the point of tears, this doesn't mean that the person is now trustworthy to come back into your life when abuse of any kind has taken place. They now need to prove they won't hurt you again. When it comes to child sexual abuse in my case, John was never to be trusted again (even though I'd forgiven him). We can't afford to risk and lose the innocence of any child, even though forgiveness has taken place. The temptation for the perpetrator is too high. As parents and caregivers, we should never trust strangers with our children's emotional and physical wellbeing. If a trusted person says they're trustworthy, we must still take care and be responsible to go slow with building trust with the stranger. Our trust is a valuable asset. Even though I believe God is merciful and gracious to every human being on earth, that doesn't warrant any abuser free right of passage to come back into our life.

The same goes with a recovering abusive alcoholic. For some people like my father, alcohol makes them angry and violent. To be around alcohol is a temptation that will bring them under the control of the alcohol again if the alcohol is in their vicinity. It takes years and years even decades of staying sober and even then, the temptation could be too high a price to pay. If they've caused pain and destruction in their relationships, then they need to build back that trust by abstaining from alcohol, and sometimes never to drink it again.

The Bible talks about forgiving seventy times seven (in other words keep on forgiving). However, we should also put boundaries in place. Yes, we need to forgive, but boundaries protect us. It's very important that we don't become blasé in our approach to abusers. If they haven't learnt from the repercussions of their crime, then they can't come back into your life.

My mum didn't put boundaries in place until it was almost too late. I've seen so many women repeat this cycle of abuse because the abuser said "sorry" but didn't change. And for some women it's been too late: they were killed by the violent acts of their abuser.

Unforgiveness can turn into bitterness, which is a horrible thing to carry. We often don't realise the impact it has on our emotional, mental and physical wellbeing. Bitterness is like being bitten by a poisonous snake: if you're going to survive, you must suck the venom out. Snake venom can affect the nervous system and paralyse the muscles and limbs. Bitterness has that effect on our bodies: it can cause so much grief and pain that our bodies begin to get sick even to the point of not being able to get out of bed. It can affect our immune system because it consumes our every thought to the point of exhaustion. It loves to rob you of a healthy life and it can rob you of valuable time being wasted on hatred. Bitterness controls us, because the person we hate is controlling our thought life and our emotional wellbeing. My thoughts were consumed entirely. I was building layers upon layers of resentment and hatred in my heart. When a person's name was mentioned, I would react and lash out from everything I was carrying in my heart.

Bitterness controls our lives and our behaviour. It controls our relationships, controls the way we parent our children and it controls the way we love our partner. It can change how we are perceived by others: from being a fun loving and caring person to a sad, angry and frustrated person carrying an angry atmosphere wherever we go.

It gets stuck on you and in you and you get stuck in it. It gets ingrained into your emotions and doesn't want to change; especially if you don't want to change or deal with the offences you carry. Bitterness likes to stay bitter: it gets comfortable being bitter and we forget that there's a better way to live when we are in this frame of mind and heart. By now you've more than likely gotten my point on what bitterness does – it's ugly!

Have you noticed that one of the most common things people say just before they die is the word "sorry," followed by "Please forgive me"? Why? Because the moment they are faced with death, they realise it's a finality of their life and they begin to regret all that was said and done.

When I apologised to my dad on the phone before he died, some people said that wasn't warranted. But for me in that moment, talking to him, I wanted him to know I wasn't above him; I was just as human as he was and have made many mistakes throughout my life. I asked him to forgive me, and he said, "It doesn't matter anymore. We are here now, talking." So much love flooded my being for him. It wasn't my own love, but God's love for him through me. This conversation would never have taken place without my faith and it would never have taken place if I didn't pick up the phone to call him. He would have died without saying a word, taking his resentment and his pain with him. It was healing for me and I hope it was healing for him. I wouldn't have had that opportunity either to say sorry. We must let the layers of unforgiveness come off us, so we can live free.

I truly believe every human being has something or someone to forgive. But human nature also loves to keep hold of those offences and grievances. We love to wallow in it, go over, drag up, argue and scream about past offences. Our hurting heart loves to live in the past, to go back and remember hurts and offences. That is when you can't forget; whereas living in forgiveness can't stay in the past. The hurt over time gets forgotten. That's why we can forgive and eventually forget.

Every time we experience an offence that we don't deal with, we build a layer and then another layer, then another layer of offence and so on. When we don't deal with those layers, it makes it easier to become more hurt again, because the wound is already open from the previous hurt. It makes sense, that when layers start to build, the love we have hidden deep within our hearts can't get through. So, the walls go up, eventually hardening our hearts towards people.

Forgiving others doesn't validate those who have hurt us and it doesn't justify their hurtful actions. Forgiveness actually saves us from a lifetime of internal pain, breaking the hold the other person has over you. For me forgiveness was about being liberated and it was about being free from the stronghold of hatred for my dad and the child molester, John. It was a gift I gave to myself and more importantly a gift I gave my husband and my children.

"Darkness cannot drive out darkness: only light can do that. Hate cannot drive out hate: only love can do that." – Martin Luther King Jr

On 17 June 2015, a tragedy occurred in Charleston, South Carolina, USA. Nine people attending a prayer meeting at the Emanuel African Methodist Church were killed by open fire enacted by a racially motivated killer. The media espoused racial hatred and white supremacy, but the church was oblivious to this. They welcomed in a man who had a deadly ulterior motive. They invited him to share in their prayer circle. A stranger was invited in. And he went on to carry out one of the deadliest mass shootings at a place of worship in the USA. This church was a place where people went to heal. It was a place where people went to experience peace within their faith and a place where people chose love over hate.

The most challenging thing emerged from this unimaginable massacre. As the killer stood in his court hearing, expressionless, family members graciously spoke forgiveness from their hearts. But so evident in their words were the grace of God's love.

"There are victims on this young man's side of the family [...] we must find it in our heart [...] to help his family as well." They chose to forgive; this was their doorway to healing. They gave him no time, no opportunity to dwell in their hearts, in their lives and no opportunity to linger and manifest through bitterness.

"They were victors in life, and champions in death." - The Emmanuel Nine

God's grace is extending the same forgiveness that God bestows on us to others.

To say "I forgive you" is being in your most vulnerable state: it's a selfless act. I deeply thought about why and how I should forgive. I thought about the consequences and I thought about all the positives it would bring as well. But the longer I left it and held onto bitterness, the more opportunity my mind had to rehearse all the painful events that had taken place and it just became harder and harder to live bitter.

Nobody I knew ever talked about forgiveness. There was never a kiss and make up atmosphere growing up. The word "sorry" was never used coinciding with a sincere heart. My parents didn't lead by example. It was common practice for Dad to blame my mum about basically everything and anything, especially everything regarding us kids. It was never my father's fault; there were no internal changes happening with them. There was no growth and there was no thought of apologising and working things out — it was all blame. I didn't want my life to be like that.

Forgiveness teaches us to search our hearts. It teaches us that life isn't always about us; it's sometimes about others. It teaches us that when someone hurts you it doesn't mean it was your fault or that it had anything to do with you in the first place. It could possibly be about what they're going through. It teaches us not to take onboard other people's problems, for e.g., our abusers' pain. It teaches us perspective, it teaches us discernment, it teaches us understanding and it grows our tendency towards compassion, empathy and understanding. Forgiveness is powerful!

I tried to find John for a few years. I wanted to confront him, I wanted to look him right in the eye and call out his depravity. I could never find where he was. Maybe he had died taking his evilness to the grave or maybe he died repenting of all the wrong he did in sincere regret. I will never know and that is OK, because I've forgiven him and been released from the pain and hurt he inflicted on me. I was unaware I was carrying so much bitterness towards him and needed to forgive him even though I couldn't tell him directly to his face and even though I would never get any form of closure from his end. When I started to unpack the sexual abuse, it all came out of my heart how much pain I had. This bitterness changed me. I was growing deeper into Melancholia, stuck in my thoughts, making myself sick. That was not who I wanted to be.

I would say, "If anyone had the right to hold onto unforgiveness, it was me." I was completely convinced of it. But I had to think of my future self. Who did I want to be in all this bitterness? Did I want to be the living dictionary definition of bitterness? Did I really want to live my life in anger, animosity, hatred and resentment? Did I want to let this bitterness eat away at my heart and mind affecting my physical wellbeing? Did I want to pass all of this hurt and pain onto my children and my husband, robbing them of what it is to truly live a gracious life? Did I want my family to get the worst of me and not the best of me? They were the questions only I could answer.

The people we hate usually don't think about us for a second of their day, meanwhile, we are consumed with them. That is bondage: you become enslaved to the person you hate and despise. You become tied to the very person you need to be free from. Please remember, forgiving someone, doesn't give them permission to come back into your life – especially someone like John. For the time I knew the man, he was untrustworthy, he was dangerous, he was predatory and he was a child molester. Even though Don wasn't a child molester, I needed to forgive him for the hurt he brought into our lives.

Just because I forgave these men, doesn't mean their behaviour was OK. It doesn't mean that I'm validating them in any way, shape or form. It doesn't mean that if I bumped into them, I'd stop them for a chat. In fact, by forgiving them I release any control they have over my life, my mind, my thoughts, my pain, my actions and my reactions. By forgiving them I see them for what they are, for what they did and I can walk straight past them with my head held high. Forgiveness breaks a harmful cycle throughout the generations. It breaks the hold bitterness has over your life. That's how powerful forgiveness is. Forgiveness is an act that is freely given, but they need to earn back that trust. Wisdom says we must be careful of letting ourselves be put in a position of being abused and hurt over and over again. They must show the evidence of change in all areas of their life.

More is Caught Than Taught a Lot of The Time

Our children have grown up watching and learning from Gary and I on how to forgive. They've seen the good, the bad and the ugly in many external situations we've faced in life together (we haven't always been the perfect example). They've seen us arguing and then saying sorry to one another. Children are a sponge; they learn from watching adults and they learn the positive and negative effects. Children when young may not be able to tell you in words how they feel, so they will act out how they feel. When my children were teenagers, they had a great habit of sitting on my bed (usually when I was just about to go to sleep), late at night talking about their day and the conversations that took place and how they felt about them. We've always given them permission to talk to us at any time of the day or night. When they unpacked their stories, often just by talking about them, it gave them a different perspective on how they felt.

Our children when growing up have had to work through the unforgiveness in their hearts towards people that have hurt them. Sometimes it's been easy and other times it's been extremely hard. They've all had friends over the years hurt them and in turn they've hurt their friends. What helps is a listening ear and a person who can advise them and give them perspective on their situation, teaching them how to forgive, asking for forgiveness and empowering them to make the decision to forgive. When children are little, they need a loving and guiding adult to help them learn to forgive, until they are at an age when you can say, "Are you're ready to forgive that person and accept their forgiveness or do you need to go and tell them you're sorry?" Perspective and understanding comes with maturity of your heart, mind and soul. But as an adult and as a parent if you harbour unforgiveness and bitterness, you can't teach your children to forgive in its entirety.

"Bear with each other and forgive one another if any of you has a grievance against someone. Forgive as the Lord forgave you." – Col 3:13

There's a saying that goes, "Hurt people, hurt people." This is the absolute truth. When we hold onto hurts, offences and grudges of any kind, we end up hurting people that we don't want to hurt – usually the ones closest to us.

Forgiveness is a lifelong journey. We will always have someone to forgive and always have someone to say sorry to, because we're not perfect human beings. We all make mistakes.

People have asked me if I found it easier to forgive one person over the other and my answer would be yes. There are people I've learnt to forgive quickly because of the nature of the offence. As I've grown and matured in my adulthood, my capacity to seek understanding, use my empathy and respond with compassion has enlarged because of forgiveness.

It's always easier to forgive when the person who has hurt you says sorry to you, but it's more courageous to say sorry to someone when they aren't willing to say sorry back. When they don't say sorry and can't see the error of their ways, that's when it becomes difficult because we want them to know how hurt we are. We want them to know how it made us feel and we want them to know the destruction it has caused us internally and externally. The only possible way we know how to do that is by remaining bitter towards them.

Don't let your bitterness become a life sentence.

Nelson Mandela had every right to hate his haters, being thrown into prison for many years for something he didn't do. And yet, he learnt to forgive. He spent twenty-seven years in prison for opposing South Africa's Apartheid system. Those twenty-seven years, he was never going to get back, but he could stop the prison sentence extending further beyond that in his life on the outside.
"As I walked out the door towards the gate that would lead to my freedom, I knew if I didn't leave my bitterness and hatred behind, I'd still be in prison." – Nelson Mandela

Forgiveness is a choice we make and I chose to forgive and making that choice myself brought me into a renewed sense of freedom. I was free from rehashing the hurts and the offences over and over again in my mind and heart, free from destructive anger and free from the deep burdens I was carrying.

Don't let unforgiveness keep you locked up emotionally and unhappiness stopping you from moving forward to enjoy your life. Don't stay in the prison of bitterness.

"If we really want to love, we must learn how to forgive." – Mother Teresa

NICOLA RUCCI

Personal Reflection

1. Do you carry unforgiveness? List the people who have hurt you over the years and what they did.

2. What events trigger unforgiveness? Do you want to continue to feel this way?

3. Do you find it hard to forgive? Why?

4. Are you ready to forgive those who have hurt you? Why?

5. Do you need to forgive yourself? Why?

6. If you pray, then pray for those who have hurt you. Ask God to help you forgive those people. Ask someone to pray with you.

7. How has this chapter helped you?

Personal Promise

If your heart is broken, you'll find God right there. If you're kicked in the gut, He'll help you catch your breath (Psalm 4:8; The Message Bible).

Sometimes rejection in life is a redirection.

Chapter 8
REJECTION IS A THIEF: IT TAKES MORE THAN IT GIVES

For God has said,

"I will never leave you nor forsake you."

Hebrews 13:5

There's a vicious cycle of rejection. You want to break free from the hold it has over you, but your rejection causes you to act as rejecter – anticipating potential rejection before it even happens. Rejection is a thief: it robs you of the love you deserve to have in your life.

Good Therapy (2023) says that rejection is the act of pushing someone or something away. In the mental health domain, rejection is associated with feelings of shame, grief and sadness.

Rejection is part of experiencing loss. We grieve when we've been rejected and its painful. For so many of us, we've experienced rejection in many areas of our lives: in a relationship with a partner through separation and/or divorce, a job loss, being told over and over again that you're not accepted for the jobs you applied for, not being invited to a party when all your other friends were invited, being bullied on the school playground and no one coming to your defence or aide, being gossiped about behind your back and people laughing and pointing fingers at you. Rejection affects your self-worth and your confidence. We react by putting up protective walls and distancing ourselves from people, in fear of being rejected again. We begin to hide what is really going on inside us.

Rejection was reinforced when Mum left us, which for her was reinforced by her own parents back in England and then again with my father and once again with the other men that came into her life (and ours); perpetuating a harmful cycle.

Rejection is a negative teacher: it taught me that I was the problem. I was the reason why she left and I wasn't lovable enough for her to stay. I would ask the question in my mind, "Why didn't she take us with her and what did we do for her to leave?" I knew why she left Dad – he tried to destroy any self-worth that she had left in her. He lost all their money, he had his fits of rage, his arrogance and his demands with his condescending words that were soul destroying. But I could never understand why she left us too. I began to build emotional walls and layers of hurt internally.

The first time I ever heard the word "rejection" was in high school. One of the girls who I was friends with was so distraught because her boyfriend broke off their relationship. She told me, "He's rejected me and doesn't want to be with me anymore." Just like that, it was like a light bulb going off in my head. I had a name for my feelings. I now knew I carried rejection. I always felt lost, alone and abandoned, like there was a loneliness embracing my soul. I always longed to have a normal family life, with loving parents. I would watch other kids interact with their parents and hoped that was me.

Many people over the years had said to me, "Who cares," "Don't worry about them," "Oh, just get over it." But you can't just get over such things. You must work through them and grow through them. Working through rejection, taught me how to overcome the hurt by people and how to love. Being rejected by the people who are close to you can be hard to understand and come to terms with. I became a people-pleaser; I needed people to like me because I never felt liked. Pleasing people gave me a false sense of security, hoping they wouldn't reject me. In being a people-pleaser, you're not secure in who you are and you never stand up for your convictions. You never have an opinion, and you certainly don't want to rock the boat, in case you become the target of being rejected again. We repeat the cycle when we become adults and work under a boss who demands you to be a "yes" person, out of fear of what they'll say about you to others.

I have a love for gardening. It's become somewhat therapeutic for me over the years. When I'm in the garden and doing the weeding, I've found that some weeds have strong roots. You must dig deep to get the weed out. You must pull the root system out, so the weed doesn't grow back again. Some weeds are easy to pull out: they're usually close to the surface of the soil and if you pull them out properly, they won't grow back again. Well, that's the idea. My husband and I have a beautiful backyard full of magnificent trees, native plants and flowers. When I don't tend to the garden as regularly as I should; I guarantee you, it won't be long before I see weeds and lots of them. They have the power to choke out the native plants and my beautiful flowers. The moment I pull the weeds out by their roots, it won't be long before my beautiful garden is flourishing again. My plants come alive when I deal with the root of the weed. That's what rejection is to us — it's like a weed with a strong root. The root gets embedded deep down in our heart and will suck the life out of us, gradually but effectively. Rejection stops us enjoying our life the way we're meant to enjoy it and we don't flourish in life the way we're meant to flourish. If we don't work through the rejection, our life can become stifled and suffocate. The bigger the weed grows, will determine how many branches of the weed there will be. There's such a tree called a "weed tree" — we have them in our backyard. These weed trees love to suck and strangle the life out of our beautiful trees. They can grow as tall as other trees. The weed trees damage the foundations of our yard and can also damage the foundations of our home. They look like they're as healthy as the other trees and even flower and bear fruit. However, when left unattended, they will kill our wonderful garden.

We've lost so many gorgeous plants in our garden because we didn't get to the weed trees before they did the damage. They spring up often very fast and camouflage themselves among the healthy flora of the garden, growing so big that they cover other plants that need to thrive. The weed tree slowly kills all the beauty in those plants, unnoticeable until it is too late. Just like a weed tree, rejection can have many branches, depending on how many people have rejected us and how we've handled the rejection. It depends on how many situations and circumstances we've been in to cause rejection, the people that neglected us, have written us off, wiped their hands of us or simply haven't cared too much about us. When you've faced these circumstances in your life and you've held onto those moments and haven't dealt with them one at a time, then they have the power to fester within you, causing you to become resentful and bitter, building layer upon layer.

To be free from the hurt and the turmoil of rejection, we need to deal with the root. Where did the rejection begin and why am I rejected by this person or persons. Some of the simple ways yet complex at the same time, is to acknowledge we all get rejected from time to time, not everybody will like us and accept us and that is OK. Processing our emotions when we feel rejected and asking ourselves the question, "Why is it making me feel the way it does?" can help put it into perspective. If it's too hard and it's affecting your home life, work life, family and friends, then that means you need to talk to someone who is qualified to help you.

Our heart is precious and doesn't belong to those who rejected us. Getting help with how you're feeling is important. It says, "I don't want to live this way anymore, I want my life to flourish; I want to be happy and full of joy." When you carry offences from people hurting you throughout your life – rejection will react and take the defensive. It makes you feel there is something wrong with you, it tells you, you are the problem even though you weren't the problem at all. But as adults working through our childhood traumas, we must take responsibility for our part we play in rejecting others, because rejected people often reject people.

Rejection cries out to be rejected.

I know it's a strange concept, but when you have layers of rejection, then rejection waits to be rejected. It sends a signal to our psyche "everyone will reject me, so I might as well do the rejecting first" or it says, "I dare you to reject me — everybody else has." All our behaviours become reactionary, failing to deal with the issue. We often think it will save us from being rejected again and giving us a sense of control over our lives. As I was working through my rejection as an adult, it taught me that I was not alone in carrying rejection, I became aware of so many other people carrying rejection, and I watched people reject each other and causing so much pain and loss.

To overcome the rejection in my life, I had to understand why I was being rejected. With my mother, she was having a nervous breakdown because of how my father was treating her. She didn't have the emotional space and energy for any of us. When I was an adult working through my trauma, I came to realise she needed to do what she had to do to survive. That brought healing for both of us.

Every time I faced rejection I would look back at the situation, who it was that rejected me and work through the forgiveness needed and find peace within myself and recognise sometimes it wasn't about me, but it was about the issues they were carrying at the time.

My father was carrying a lot of pain from his childhood. Did that excuse him from being a neglectful abusive father? No. Did that excuse him from being an alcoholic and destroying our family unit? No. But for me, again, it made sense as to why he was the way he was. That is perspective. I could forgive him for rejecting me and being hurtful. That is maturity.

I stopped blaming myself when I had perspective of all the situations I grew up in as a child. I started to focus on what I was good at and who I wanted to become in my life and move forward into the plans and purpose for me and my family.

Sometimes rejection in life is a redirection.

NICOLA RUCCI

Personal Reflection

1. Do you feel rejected, ignored and disregarded by some people? Who are those people?

2. Why do you feel rejected by them?

3. Do you also reject people? Why do you push them away?

4. Do you have friends? Who are they? Ask yourself why they are your friends.

5. In which way has this chapter helped you?

Personal Promise(s)

God will never reject me. God said He would never leave me nor forsake (abandon) me (Hebrews 13:5).

Even though my parents may have abandoned me, He says He will never forget me, in fact, He has carved me on the palm of His hand like a tattoo (Isaiah 49:16).

Jesus said we aren't orphans; we are His children, and He gives us the Holy Spirit to guide us and to comfort us (John 14:18).

Shame carries secrets and shame fears those secrets being exposed.

Chapter 9
SHAME CARRIES SECRETS

"Shame derives its power from being unspeakable."
Brené Brown

Throughout my life, the power of secrets had to be broken. The secrets that were hiding in the dark had to come into the light, so that they would no longer have any hold over me.

Shame loves to isolate your negative thought patterns and it feeds on the loneliness of your heart. My world suddenly opened to a whole new level of depravity at such a young age. John (like most child molesters who indirectly confess to their paedophilia) told me, "This is our secret and no one, especially not your mother, can know." John was a creepy man. He used to look at me in a sly, manipulating and controlling way – it instilled fear within me.

This was evil and brought more fear into my young world than living with the unpredictability of my dad's drinking. This was eviler than the shouting and fighting that I saw and experienced. It was premeditated evil: he'd plan his nights coming into my bedroom and I knew that plan – it kept me awake, never knowing when the door was about to open.

The fear of watching Mum get beaten shut my mouth. The fear of watching my brother get beaten shut my mouth. The fear of what my father would do in his drunken state also kept my mouth shut. Shame thrives on fear keeping its secrets.

We all carried shame throughout our young lives, and so did my mother. Mum was always feeling bad about our childhood and always feeling guilty about the circumstances we were in. The guilt really sunk in when we were all adults. Mum often said, "It's all my fault for how you all turned out." She'd relive the trauma in her mind of what we went through repeatedly and go down a victim spiral. I remember saying to her, "We all have a choice to become better versions of ourselves or go down a destructive path. You chose to become a better version of yourself, Mum."

After many years and following the birth of our first two children, my brother approached me at a family barbecue about what John did to me. So much time had passed and it really shocked me that he even knew and remembered what John did to me. I hadn't told anyone other than Mum about the abuse.

David had only seen that one night and in his mind he thought I allowed John to do what he did to me. I sat down with him and explained that I didn't allow any of that to happen. I told John to stop and even if I hadn't told him to stop, I couldn't have. I was a child and he was a huge man. David just couldn't believe it and said, "Why didn't anyone help you?" The question is why no one helped any of us, for that matter. I told David that I was so scared to say anything because of who John was. I felt all alone. David asked me why I didn't fight back and why I didn't scream out for help.
I don't know why I didn't fight back then; I don't know why I didn't kick and scream and yell at the top of my voice

and I don't know why I didn't punch him. But I do know it wasn't my fault: he was the perpetrator of abuse and I was the victim. I was a child and full of fear.

Shame hides in the dark and it feeds off of isolation and loneliness.

Both my sister and my brother carried their own shame, but my brother also carried my shame and made it his. He was scared to say something when we were young so he buried it deep within him, like I did. If he hadn't have said something to me that day at the barbecue, I would never have had the opportunity to bring what John did to us into the open and clear things up with him.

Shame carries secrets and shame fears those secrets being exposed.

Nobody knew what I was going through internally: not my parents, my grandparents, my brother or sister; teachers, or even school friends. I never spoke about my home life and traumatic experiences. I only started speaking up once I became an adult.

I was always fearful of what people would think of me and I saw myself in a negative light. When the people closest to me would say things about me to others, I would then assume that everybody must think the same things of me: this is what shame does. Shame puts labels on you. It calls you an idiot, stupid, dumb, failure, useless, ugly, and says you'll never amount to anything in your life. According to the Merriam-Webster Dictionary, the word shame means, "a painful emotion caused by consciousness of guilt, shortcoming or impropriety."

To illustrate: When people gossip and speak badly about you behind your back, mocking your weaknesses and who you are, then in turn those people who have listened to those words about you can think the same things. You then get embarrassed and feel humiliated even though the words they've said about you aren't true. That brings shame and with shame comes guilt, thinking you are at fault. Then comes condemnation, making you feel you're of no worth.

I would speak negative words over my life; like "dumb," "stupid," or "useless" continually, reinforcing their negativity and power, because they were spoken to me. Every time someone got angry at me or something hard would come up at school, I would say I'm dumb or stupid and I can't do it (when in actual fact I could and I wasn't dumb or stupid at all). The negativity of those words wanted to stop me from learning to push through and persevere in the moment. The hold shame has on you, breaks the moment you get the courage to speak the secrets out and expose the lies. When shame speaks out, the truth is exposed.

Words are powerful: they can bring life or death to your soul. They have the power to damage you for the rest of your life; robbing you of who you really are, robbing you of who you were created to be and robbing you of living in the freedom of your life. Or they can bring healing, comfort and strength; lifting your heart and mind to be the best version of yourself.

When we say things in the heat of the moment, we don't recognise the damage it has actually caused. We can't take back those words. When we speak out in anger or frustration, the moment the words leave our mouth, they've caused the damage. Many of us have said things when we're angry; they are mean and awful words. We say them because we're hurting and we want the person to hurt just as bad as we're hurting. We use our words as weapons to deliberately bring the other person down, to cause them to crumble, to inflict pain on them and the same pain that we feel. The Bible says, "Death and life are in the power of the tongue." – Proverbs 18:21

Those hurtful words we speak are soul destroying; not just to our own heart but to those around us as we lash out. If we can recognise what's going on in our heart before we say hurtful words, then we can eliminate the damage it will cause.

"Out of the abundance of the heart, the mouth speaks." This is so true: that's why it's important for healing to take place in our hearts (Matthew 12:34-40).

When I was in my early twenties and unpacking my shame, I had to acknowledge why I felt shame, guilt and condemnation; naming those things that were hidden deep down in my spirit and bringing them into the light. It's good to talk to a trusted person or to someone that can hold your heart safely (like I explained in the Vulnerability chapter). We need to share our hearts with people who care about us and who have our best interest at heart.

NICOLA RUCCI

Personal Reflection

1. Do you personally feel shame when certain people say things about you? What words hurt you the most?

2. Do certain people hurt you more than others? Why?

3. Do you think their comments about you are true? Why?

4. What can you say about yourself to counteract such feelings of shame?

5. How has this chapter helped you?

Personal Promise

God, you accept me even when I do and think the wrong things.

You know everything about me God. You created my innermost being (Psalm 139:13-14).

Restored people help others in their journey to restoration.

Chapter 10
OUR HEALING JOURNEY ISN'T A RACE TO THE FINISH LINE

Stop and breathe: it's OK to take your time and slow down.

"He refreshes my soul. He guides me along the right paths, for His name's sake. Even though I walk through the darkest valley, I will fear no evil; for You are with me. Your rod and staff, they will comfort me." – Psalm 23:3-4

We were never meant to stay in the valley; in the darkness, the pain, the turmoil, and the grief of our experiences. The passage above says, "As I walk through the darkest valley." That's right – it's a walk-through; not a destination. It's not a place we were meant to camp out in forever. It's a place that's meant to give us hope, because we'll get through it.

God wants to restore the years that were taken from you. Restoration is defined as the act of returning something to its former condition; it's the making of something new again. The Greek word for restoration means reclamation, restitution, reinstatement and a settlement day.

To be restored is to bring something back to its rightful place or its rightful condition. My husband bought me my very first car: it was a 1965 Ford Cortina. He bought it for five hundred Australian dollars in 1985. He restored it back to its natural beauty. It had crushed velvet seats and a beautiful new blue glossy paint job. The engine was brand new again. It was such a great car to drive. He took something that was doomed for the junk yard and made it new again, by striping it back to its raw state.

When we begin the restoration process, it will feel like we're being exposed again: we will feel raw and uncomfortable. That raw state is getting to the root issues of our trauma and that's a good thing. It's like when you have an infected cut: the cut needs to be cleaned out with warm salty water and then the antiseptic cream applied and either it needs to be covered over with a bandage or left exposed so the air can heal it.

I couldn't begin to help others if I myself didn't heal from the anger, the bitterness, the hurt, the shame, the guilt and the condemnation of my youth. As I embraced my healing journey, I was able to rely on my faith. God's unfailing love for my life was that same love that carried me through my grief. I could see a future of fulfilment and joy in my life. I had to work hard at it and as painful as that journey was, I persevered through it all. It was up to me to listen to wise counsel and take onboard why I was the way I was, why I thought the way I thought about myself and why I reacted to situations like I did.

It took time to see myself the way I should: fun loving and full of love, life and joy and that's OK. Stop and breathe: it's not a race to the finish line; it's a walk. Sometimes it's a sit-down and sometimes it's someone holding your hand as you just rest.

And just when you think it will take forever, you wake up one day with a different perspective on your life and on who you are.

It helped to be connected to people who believed in me and didn't reject me and who loved me for who I was. Love definitely helps our healing journey and the countless Bible studies I was involved in, the support and love of a friend that never gave up on me, when everyone else did, all contributed. The scriptures I read every day began to have a positive effect on my mind and my emotions and in turn made a positive impact on my immediate family. My mind was being renewed and my thinking reframed; giving me hope and a new understanding of my purpose in life. People began to see the difference in me. My personality actually changed from being negative and very melancholy to outgoing and happy. My heart softened with a greater understanding of the love I was reading about in the scriptures.

As I've gotten older, my appreciation for life is expressed in my gardening, in my friendships and close family, in how I advise people who are going through trials of all sorts, telling them that they will get through this, giving them hope and loving them along the way.

Restored people help others in their journey to restoration.

"Your people will rebuild the ancient ruins and will raise up the age-old foundations; you will be called Repairer of Broken Walls, Restorer of streets and dwellings." – Isaiah 58:12

This scripture doesn't necessarily mean we'll repair actual buildings or rebuild their foundations. It often means that we'll play a part in helping our family, friends, neighbours, work colleagues to be healed and be restored. It means we're to play our part in helping them build new foundations in their life so that, in turn, their new foundations are strong, stable and secure. It'll take work to rebuild our life and support others to rebuild their lives (just like it takes hard work to rebuild broken down walls from building structures). For our life to have meaning and purpose and longevity we need to do the work on the inside first, the infrastructure of our souls.

Give yourself some time and room to heal and restore from life's tragedies. Life is precious and our lives are precious and it's up to us to embrace life – a life of healing, comfort and restoration.

The Bible says that hope is an anchor to our souls – the hope we find in Christ.

Hope is a very powerful word and when we put hope in its rightful place, then we stay steady and secure. I have held onto hope in God; a hope that this world cannot give me and a hope that no government body can give me. It's hope that doesn't let go of me. It's a hope that anchors my soul and doesn't waver when I'm faced with tough times. This hope is a knowing deep down within my heart that I am in my Father's hands.

When I add up the layers of trauma in my life, I never thought it was even possible to begin the journey of healing and restoration. Just like my friend who was seventy years old, age has no barrier to healing. You can start your journey at any age, at anytime and anywhere: you just need to want to.

Personal Reflection

1. What are some areas of your life that you know needs to slow down?

2. Do you have people in your life to advise you to pause and reflect?

3. Do you have hope? What does that look like?

4. How has this chapter helped you?

Personal Promise

God, You are my hope and strength today (Philippians 4:13).

This hope I have is an anchor for my soul, both sure and steadfast (Hebrews 6:19).

God, fill me with all joy and peace today as I believe that I may abound in hope by the Holy Spirit (Romans 15:13).

NICOLA RUCCI

Chapter 11
WHAT HELPED ME, MAY HELP YOU

In this chapter I want to share a few of the practical things that have really helped me on my healing journey. Perhaps they will help you too.

Journaling

Journaling has become one of my habits. When I was dealing with my trauma, I would buy a notebook and I write down how I was feeling and thinking. I would also write down my reflections and thoughts after I read the bible. I didn't write everyday – only when I was up for it. When I didn't feel like talking to people, I'd write instead. Reading back my words months later, helped me gain an understanding of who I was in that season, how far I had progressed, and enabled me to keep walking through the issues.

Slowing down

Don't be influenced by everyone else wanting to rush you. Relax the process of your grief and healing, instead of keeping to a timeline. Take the pressure off yourself. I came to understand our healing journey doesn't have a deadline. When everyone around us is in a hurry, and wanting us to work to their agenda, we need to be determined to say no. Give yourself permission to heal over time.

Being busy

Well just after I said to slow down, I'm now saying that keeping busy sometimes helps as well. I know it sounds a little crazy but dare I say it, sometimes keeping busy helped me to have a break from my grief. Going back to work eventually and being around my colleagues again, all contributed to me regaining a sense of purpose. Sometimes our circumstances and our grief can drain us of so much emotional energy: we need to get back to making a difference in our world. But again, we are all on our own unique journey. How something helps one person may not help another.

Happy Place

I use to make time to go to the place I loved; and that is the ocean. It's still my happy place! Gary and I call it 'ocean therapy'. When we lived in Adelaide, I would go down to the Glenelg Beach and just sit on the sand watching the waves go in and out. Alternatively, I would go to Moana beach, near my mother's house. You can take your car onto the beach, right down near the ocean. Sometimes I just sat and watched the families having their fun with each other in the water. Or I would chat with the local fisherman: we would have some great conversations. In Brisbane, I go to the Sunshine Coast and find a nice spot in Caloundra or go to the amazing Mooloolaba Beach. These are great places to relax and take in the beautiful scenery, to smell the sea water and put my feet into the hot sand. These moments my mind off the pressures of the past and present. Being with friends that make you laugh and with loved ones who hold your hand, are medicine to the soul.

We all need to find that place that helps the healing process - a place where we can reflect on our own life. It might be going to the mountains, going hiking, fishing, or four-wheel driving. Your happy place could be in your garden, sitting and listening to the birds sing or sitting by the pool.

Nutrition

There is a saying 'You are what you eat'. There is some truth to this. During my journey I needed to take care of myself. A friend of mine asked me whether I was eating after I'd lost my brother. I had lost weight. I told them it was the last thing I felt like doing. Food is medicine for our bodies. I realised that if I didn't keep eating properly, then it would affect my mind and emotions and eventually affect our family. I realised a poor diet would affect my energy levels which I needed to look after my kids and my husband. Takeaway food had its place of convenience and comfort for a little while, but long term it is not conducive to good health. For our family, home cooking is always best.

Activity

It is good to stay active. My love for running not only kept me fit but it also helped my mental health while healing and grieving. Some days I would just put on my jogging shoes and run for ages. To this day, running continues to help me to lower my stress levels and maintain a clear mind. Exercise of any sort (like walking, running, hiking, golf or playing some sport) is known to help our mental health and keep us physically fit. Doing any activity is healthy for us – like drawing, painting, reading, doing puzzles, going to the gym, joining an art group, learning a hobby, or volunteering to help people in need. All these can go a long way to helping us on our healing journey.

Make Time with Good Friends

Building quality friendships is so important as we heal. The bible says, if you want friends be friendly. Reach out. Be courageous. Don't lock yourself away. Friendships that care for you, listen to you, and encourage you are a breath of fresh air. We all need friends like that.

Prayer and Meditation

While I am a big believer in getting help from our medical professionals and holistic therapies to support us in our healing journey, as a Christian, I also pray to my Heavenly Father. My faith in God has been my constant source of strength throughout my life since I was eighteen years old. My faith reminds me that there's hope for my life. It helps me to rely on something much bigger than I am, and much bigger than what I'm going through and have been through. As I've walked through the heartache and pain, my faith has also helped me get through it.

I often spend time praying not just for myself but for others who are experiencing their own trials. I would pray for my family who are struggling, taking the focus off myself. Prayer helped me focus on (and still helps me focus on) what other people are going through. It didn't downplay my emotional grief, but it helped me gather my emotions better. As I drew close to God, God would draw close to me, and would give me strength in my time of need.

Sitting, relaxing, and doing absolutely nothing, refreshes my soul. When I go to the beach and sit there watching the waves come in and out, it's therapeutic for my mind and body. When I begin to think about God and His promises for my life, it is therapeutic for my spirit. These are forms of meditation.

Listening to music that uplifts my heart and mind has also helped my healing journey. Worship can be powerful. Songs with lyrics that glorify Jesus are soothing, calming, and healing.

These are some of the things that have helped me in my healing journey.

Personal Reflection

1. Are there things you need to stop saying "yes" to?

2. Do you have a happy place that relaxes and refreshes your mind and heart?

3. Can you make time to do something that is rewarding to others?

4. How has this chapter helped you?

Personal Promise

What is your personal promise to yourself?

> *We can't change where we've been, but we can certainly change where we're going.*

Chapter 12
MY FAITH

"From the end of the earth I will cry to You. When my heart is overwhelmed, lead me to the Rock that is higher than I."

Psalm 61:2

Even though my childhood trauma had shaped so much of my young life, it didn't define who I am today. I chose to be defined by who I am in God's eyes. We can't change where we've been, but we can certainly change where we're going.

My faith was one of the things that helped support me in my healing journey. It began when I took responsibility for my future self and stepped into my pain, embracing Gods love for my life. I couldn't have gotten through without God's grace and love; a loving husband by my side and the few people who believed in me. My faith in a loving and gracious God and incredible friendships gave me the courage to step into my pain and confront my fears and doubts.

As I began my relationship with God, I came to understand that He is indeed a loving and gracious God. He is Grace and gracious; not mean, nasty or an angry God as it was portrayed to me all my young life. His grace isn't something He gives or removes depending on His mood. God's grace is constant because God embodies grace. I believe I exist because of God's grace and I am saved from my past by His grace.

When I studied the word grace, I discovered in the Old Testament, the original Hebrew word is the verb 'khanan', and in the Greek New Testament the original word is 'charis'. Both words carrying the meaning of favour, goodwill and loving-kindness: a kindness which is bestowed upon someone who doesn't deserve it. A grace that I didn't deserve. The people in my life who hurt me didn't deserve my forgiveness either, but grace says: "Forgive them."

Someone once criticised my faith, and said it was 'just a crutch to lean on', because only lame people need a crutch. I responded, "Oh well, if you want to put it that way, then yes, my faith is a crutch! I am weak and I rely on my faith in God. Believing in a loving heavenly Father makes so much more sense to me than relying on alcohol, drugs, gambling, sex, or pornography to fill the void in my heart that I knew was there." Usually, people who make such comments are finding ways to deal with their own pain and often fail.

C.S. Lewis wrote, "We may ignore, but we can nowhere evade, the presence of God. The world is crowded with Him."

I knew God was real. He was always with me, no matter where I went or whatever situation I faced.

Research says that a person's faith helps their overall wellbeing.

My faith didn't take all my problems away, but it gave me the strength to face my hurt and deal with my struggles. It took time to overcome the abuse I experienced and there were many times in the early years when the fears would come flooding back. But I was reminded every single time through the Bible that God was with me, He was for me and wouldn't leave me.

John 16:33 says, "These things I have spoken to you, that in Me you may have peace. In the world you will have tribulation; but be of good cheer; I have overcome the world."

I grew in confidence because I knew He was with me in my troubles. Peace and happiness were real possibilities for me, because He was helping me overcome my fears.

Another scripture that gave me hope and spoke to my heart when I was eighteen, is Philippians 1:6, it says, "Being confident of this very thing, that He (God) who has begun a good work in you will complete it until the day of Jesus Christ."

I instantly knew in my heart that it was possible to complete my healing journey with a loving and gracious God at my side. A God who had forgiven me of all my wrongdoings (sins), who would never forget me or abandon me, and who would stay with me to the very end. As the years passed by, He gave me the strength to overcome my traumatic past. However, I had to agree with God's word and allow Him to direct my path. When God begins something, he promises to finish it. He doesn't leave us 'high and dry' halfway through His perfect work in us. But we must cooperate with God. We can't quit because it's too hard. There is no denying it is hard, but by God's amazing grace, strength, comfort, and counsel, we will get through those painful times. As I reflect on the past, I know I would not have come through without God and some incredible people walking alongside me..

As a child and as a young adult, I was fearful and insecure. Fear makes you anxious, nervous, and scared. This type of fear is a thief: it's a taker and it doesn't give you anything of worth. It doesn't add value to your life; it just takes. It steals your hope, it robs your joy, and it destroys your confidence. It reduces your personhood. Fear thrives on fear. So, to overcome fear I learned to read the scriptures in the Bible that told me not to fear: they reminded me of hope and love and safety.

In Isaiah 41:10 it says, "Fear not, for I am with you; be not dismayed, for I am your God. I will strengthen you, yes, I will help you, I will uphold you with my righteous right hand."

This was yet another scripture that gave me hope. These words comforted me in every fearful situation. Like a song on replay, negative words from the past were repeated in my mind. So I began to speak back at those negative words with scripture. I started to change the way I spoke about myself. One by one, I began to overcome the impact of those negative thoughts.

As I continued to read the bible, I was constantly learning this new life of faith in God. I began to live more confidently as I experienced the power of Living by faith and not by fear. It took a lot of perseverance and patience, because I desperately wanted to overcome my past. A warrior spirit grew within me. Even though I was a feisty young woman a lot of that emotion stemmed from the desire to protect myself. Now it was different, I knew God was protecting me! The Holy Spirit put a fight within me that said "I'm not going to quit, I'm not giving up, I will overcome". As I leaned more upon the scriptures, they reframed my mind and emotions. I felt more and more of His power within in me and my faith strengthening daily.

"Fight the good fight of faith, lay hold on eternal life, to which you were also called and confessed the good confession in the presence of many witnesses." – 1 Timothy 6:12

Nobody drifts through life trouble-free. Our lives are loaded with trails, heartaches, testing times, and uphill battles. This scripture reminds me that no matter what comes my way: I can stay strong, trust and believe. I can pray and not give up hope and see it through until the very end. All the while knowing that God who loves me, was always right beside me.

"I have fought the good fight; I have finished the race and I have kept the faith." - 2 Timothy 4:7

The scriptures have always helped me to stay strong in my faith and not quit when life gets too hard. They remind me to remain strong in faith and to allow my foundation and roots grow deeper into all the things God wants for my life. The scriptures give me fresh meaning, new purpose, continual learning and sometimes answers to my questions (and I say sometimes because not everything will have an answer in our life). The scriptures remind me to talk to the people who can help me, seek wise counsel, to persevere, endure, persist and to never run away or hide from my challenges or lean towards things that bring harm to me or my family.

Our negative thoughts often lie to us about ourselves.

I would often put myself down, and tell myself I was worthless, useless and stupid; my mind would wander down a dark negative pathway. My mind struggled to understand what was happening. I didn't know how to overcome the challenges of my past. When I was able to recognise the patterns of my thinking, I was positioned to understand and control my emotions better.

Every day we are bombarded with negativity, which only compound the dark thoughts from the past. Reading the bible showed me how loved I was, and it gave me hope in the hopeless outlook of my life.... Even though it took a lot of strength and perseverance to push through, I overcome the negativity one lie at a time. My faith in God has guided me through each step of my painful journey. I am completely delivered from my past experiences and transformed me into the woman I am today. I believe God's word is truly miraculous.

Isaiah 61:1-3 says, "The Spirit of the Lord God is upon Me, for the Lord has anointed Me to preach good tidings to the poor, He has sent Me to heal the broken hearted, to proclaim liberty to the captives and the opening of the prison to those who are bound; to proclaim the acceptable year of the Lord and the day of vengeance of our God; to comfort all who mourn, to give them beauty for ashes, the oil of joy for mourning, the garment of praise for the spirit of heaviness."

We do not need to stay in the prison of our pain, anger, rejection, addictions, shame, and bitterness. Why? Because Jesus can set you free, by opening those prison doors. The Psalmist said He heals the brokenhearted and bandages our wounds. He wants us to live free and help those who are still bound by their hurt and pain.

If you decide to trust God today and surrender your hurt, pain and unforgiveness to Him, He will restore back to you all those things that were stolen from you. It won't happen in an instant, but it will happen over time if you trust Him. You don't need to allow your hurt and pain to have the final way in your life. God will turn things around for you if you surrender to Him.

Even though God can use us in the midst of our messy lives, it is more powerful when God helps us overcome our mess and empower us to help others get unstuck from their past trauma. Our miracle is passed to others needing a miracle; our life's miraculous message can become someone else's miraculous message. That's how God works: He restores us so others can be restored.

This is what my relationship with God has taught me.

"Are you tired? Worn out? Burned out on religion? Come to Me. Come away with Me and you'll recover your life. I'll show you how to take a real rest. Walk with Me and work with Me: watch how I do it. Learn the unforced rhythms of grace. I won't lay anything heavy or ill-fitting on you. Keep company with Me and you'll learn to live freely and lightly." – The Message Bible Matt 11:28-30

The Bible also says that as we draw near to God, He will draw near to us. It's a promise: God keeps His promises.

Would you pray this prayer with me today?

Lord, I surrender to you all of the pain, the hurt, the bitterness, the rejection, the shame, the guilt and the condemnation that happened to me and that I've held onto. Today, Lord, I give it all over to You, so that You can have Your perfect way in my heart, my mind and my emotions. I thank You, Lord for opening the prison doors of my heart and for taking me on my journey of healing and restoration. I know Lord, that it won't be easy as I walk through my mess, but I know You will be with me every step of the way. I thank you Lord that I can get through all I went through with Your amazing grace over my life. I will trust you Lord, with the process of my healing journey, Amen.

I celebrate with you today and my prayer is that you will find hope and freedom in Christ Jesus.

Lots of love,

Nicola

INVISIBLE SCARS

NICOLA RUCCI

ABOUT THE AUTHOR

Nicola has been a pastor, leader, communicator and respected prophetic voice for more than three decades both in Australia and the UK. She is passionate about discipleship and helping people overcome barriers to personal growth. Together with her husband, Nicola leads Rivercity Family Church, Brisbane, Australia: a traditional church becoming a network of Micro-churches and Missional Communities. They have also served in a few of Australia's megachurches and held portfolios with the National Leadership Team of Assemblies of God Great Britain. Nicola is the proud mother of three adult children, Steffany, Christopher and Jonathan.

Manufactured by Amazon.com.au
Sydney, New South Wales, Australia